The Insanity Machine

The Insanity Machine

Life with Paranoid Schizophrenia

Kenna McKinnon

with Austin Mardon, PhD, CM

Copyright (C) 2012 Kenna McKinnon
Layout design and Copyright (C) 2017 Creativia
Published 2017 by Creativia (www.creativia.org)
ISBN: 978-1548154226
Cover art by Cover Mint

Contents

Introduction   1

Acknowledgements   4

Chapter 1: Our Stories   5

Chapter 2: Defining Schizophrenia   27

Chapter 3: Treating Schizophrenia   47

Chapter 4: The Role of Environment in Schizophrenia   52

Chapter 5: Spirituality   63

Chapter 6: Stigma and Harassment   70

Chapter 7: The Perception of Violence   75

Chapter 8: Financial Concerns   80

Chapter 9: Seniors with Schizophrenia   84

Chapter 10: Living Accommodations   92

Chapter 11: Homelessness   98

Chapter 12: Activities and Hobbies   104

Chapter 13: The Role of Stress   112

Chapter 14: Medications   118

Chapter 15: Mentoring   123

Chapter 16: Safety and Supervision   125

Chapter 17: Finding joy and meaning while living with
      schizophrenia   129

Chapter 18: Final thoughts   132

Resources   135

Caregiving/Self Care Checklist   137

Afterword   140

About The Authors   141

References   144

To my children

Introduction

Awake! for Morning in the Bowl of Night
Has flung the Stone that puts the Stars to Flight:
And Lo! the Hunter of the East has caught
*The Sultan's Turret in a Noose of Light.**
*The Rubaiyat of Omar Khayyam, Verse 1, translation by
Edward Fitzgerald

This book is called *The Insanity Machine* because in 1978, Kenna
McKinnon chatted with another inmate in the old 5C forensic psychiatry ward at Alberta Hospital Edmonton and determined to write
it someday. Today the book is written as planned in 1978. It had
many setbacks and at least two professionals promised to write it with
Kenna, but withdrew before any further commitments were made.
Today, Austin Mardon and Kenna Mary McKinnon join memories and
talents to bring into the light a mental illness that was shoved into a
dark attic only a generation ago, and often today as well. That illness
is called schizophrenia. Both Kenna and Austin have a form of the
illness called paranoid schizophrenia, characterized by delusions, hallucinations and withdrawal from reality. They have been successfully
treated and both live different but useful and meaningful lives.

1

The purpose of our stories is to offer hope to those who read this book, and elucidation to those ignorant of the wonders and ravages of mental illness; to those employers, friends and family who misunderstood us and our fellow travelers. To bring understanding to those who told Kenna she was "bad" or "weak," those who didn't understand the consequences of a serious mental disorder that turned a pile of clothing into snakes and chased Kenna's subconscious into labyrinths of Hell and images of the Devil for 20 years of her initial illness; to those who advised Austin to undergo sterilization within three months of his diagnosis, and who interfered with his decision to marry in 2006 because presumably they thought he didn't have the capacity to make that decision.

Kenna has three children, all caring, intelligent, independent adults who contribute to society in their own awesome way. She raised the two younger herself, with the help of family members after she became ill. Gratitude is given especially to her brother Byron, and his wife Diane, who quit her job to care for the two children when Kenna first became magnificently and sporadically psychotic. The children may bear the scars today but don't show them, because of the strength of their genes and perhaps the love that was there but often hidden, their own innate honesty and goodness, perhaps even because of their early struggles which led to compassion, courage and strength. They are good and healthy adults.

The eldest child, raised by loving adoptive parents, is also a delight. Living sometimes with his own demons with a faith that is foreign to Kenna's family, he was born when Kenna was 17 years old and unable to raise her new baby at the time; he was placed by the Salvation Army in a loving adoptive family. Their faith, his upbringing, and also his genes have made him strong, gentle and compassionate.

This book was not always easy to write. We won't bore you, the reader, with useless details but will go right into our stories, and the story of schizophrenia in our country today and yesterday, in our cities and individual homes—even the streets, hospitals and jails.

There will be some statistics and particularly many anecdotes gleaned especially by Austin from acquaintances and friends over 19 years. He has been an advocate for others who haven't always had the success we have enjoyed and so he has heard their stories. Kenna made this journey mostly on her own by her choice since she first became ill in 1975. Contact with others like her or even those who might understand was limited until now.

We're thankful that we live in Canada where medical treatment is provided at no charge to the consumer. We're thankful for those who understand. We're thankful for those with bipolar illness, anxiety disorders, depression, obsessive-compulsive disorder, dementia, autism, and all the other forms taken by what mental health professionals label as mental illness. Thank God for you all, and the professionals who successfully and compassionately treat us. Bless the homeless who sleep by the curb, thank God for our own warm beds and good food, and a roof over our heads at night. We're thankful for health at last.

There are many people we haven't mentioned. We have been angry. We have been abused and misunderstood. Ignorance and fear have reared their monstrous hydra heads all too frequently throughout our adult lives. We come from dysfunctional backgrounds. We are children of God but have been disrespected and sometimes treated as refuse, and by those very institutions and people who purport to help those who cannot help themselves. We have also been held and protected, and given chances that others like us do not have. Employers have been understanding. Friends and family have often provided support. We found a religious faith and we've walked with gods. We are grateful for this.

Despite the disappointments and occasional anger, this book was written with love and compassion. Enter its doors and see for yourself. Feel the light on your head. It's the story of one percent of our world's population and our walk with Schizophrenia.

Acknowledgements

Judith Hansen is a friend and editor who has thoughtfully and intelligently edited this book. We commend her for her thoroughness and patience; however, Austin and Kenna take responsibility for any omissions or errors in the manuscript. Without Judi's professionalism and friendship, the book would not be the finished product it is.

We also acknowledge our friends, family, co-workers, doctors, nurses, the legal system, therapists and the Schizophrenia Society of Alberta for insights, love, support and patience over the years, without which we would not be the people we are today.

Chapter 1:
Our Stories

"Ah, but a man's reach should exceed his grasp, or what's a heaven for?" - Robert Browning
(*or* **woman's** - *our note*)

Religious delusions are common symptoms of schizophrenia. Kenna McKinnon's illness was somewhat typical in this respect. The year was 1975; the year of the demons when her schizophrenia first began to make itself evident.

Kenna Wild (Kenna) huddled in the corner of her rented townhouse, leafing through the pages of an old Bible that screamed obscenities at her. She was sure the Devil was in the room. Nothing made sense. A pile of laundry in the kitchen had writhed and turned into snakes. Music from a tape on the stereo mocked her with vulgar rhymes. She recalled a muddy and torn comic book she had found on the street one fall. It concerned a youth group investigating a demonic church, and had instructions for such an event.

Kenna glanced down at the Bible in her hands. She opened it at random, where it fell open to Revelations 3:20. *"Behold I stand at the door and knock, if anyone hears my voice and opens the door, I will come into him and dine with him and he with me...*" The phrase had been underlined in red by the teacher who had given Kenna the book as a child, and the words flashed at her now like a neon sign. It was the only verse which made sense. The young woman felt a sense of sudden elation. Perhaps there was a way from the Pit, from the driving presence of the Devil within her? "Jesus Christ, save my soul," Kenna said out loud.

The Bible lay open in her hands. She felt a sense of calm. Hesitantly at first, she leafed through the book, reading first one verse then another. The words fell into place, all making sense, all with a surety of strength and power that Kenna knew would overcome the evil Forces within her soul.

At various times Kenna would bless a glass of water from the kitchen tap and sprinkle this "Holy Water" on the chest of an invisible Devil standing in the room next to her. She saw the drops of water bounce off the Devil's chest. At other times, she would walk barefoot and coatless in the snow outside her townhouse, seeing the Devil's mocking face in the clouds above, and hordes of demons following Him through the sky. The Devil wore a classic goatee and horns, but with the most sensuous mouth Kenna had ever seen. She knew that mouth had sucked at her on many nights when she lay half asleep in her bed, attacked by demons and the Devil himself.

So it began. The nightmare of mental illness. A caring acquaintance called a psychologist at Student Counseling Services at the University of Alberta in 1975 where Kenna was a graduating student that year. Kenna received counseling once a week for two to three years, but remained unmedicated for that period of time, frightened, violent at times, and increasingly ill.

In 1978 Kenna was in trouble with the law for uttering threats and trespassing. She was sent to the Forensic Unit of Alberta Hospital Edmonton, a forensic psychiatric institution, where she was diagnosed for the first time with paranoid schizophrenia. Psychotropic medication at that time was in its infancy. She received an antidepressant as well as a tranquilizer and Chlorpromazine, another major tranquilizer, with side effects so severe that she could not get a fork or cup to her mouth without spilling due to the shaking of her hands. She could not climb stairs due to dizziness and fatigue resulting from the heavy doses of medication she was given.

After her release, neighbors would take her to picnics and Kenna would fall asleep on the picnic table, being unable to stay awake for more than half an hour at a time. She continued to drive her car (a neon green Dodge frighteningly called a Demon). One day she drove out to the country at a high speed with the intent to crash her car into a cliff. Listening to a sympathetic DJ and music on the car radio calmed her, and she drove home without incident. She was at frequent risk of suicide at that time, on another occasion lining up her pills and bottles of wine with lethal intent, rescued by a friend she had the foresight to call.

Kenna's husband had died in 1971. She was left with two small children who were forced to move often during their childhood due to Kenna's instability. She raised the children as well as she could but with difficulty, and they were intermittently cared for by friends and family.

Kenna began smoking and abusing alcohol in 1978. She quit smoking the summer of 1985. She quit drinking alcohol in June 1993. Without these interventions, she is certain she would be dead by now.

She is also certain her children bear the scars of living with the years of their mother's mental illness. She didn't abuse them physically but now feels keenly their emotional and physical neglect by her at that time.

An unhappy marriage followed in 1982, terminated by divorce in 1987. Kenna and her children lived in rented apartments thereafter, and she worked as much as possible throughout those difficult years. Her daughter left home after graduation from high school at age 17 and put herself through University with Distinction. Kenna's son attended NAIT and received a diploma in Telecommunications while working full-time as well. Her son lived at home with Kenna during that time.

One night he came home and found Kenna had thrown all his records and most of the canned goods in the home into the dumpster. They had come from the Devil, she said. Her son patiently explained that Kenna was free to throw away her own possessions if she wished, but please to leave his alone. He rescued what he could from the dumpster that night.

Her children, friends and neighbors and frequent appointments with a psychiatrist and other professionals were to be her major sources of emotional support. A minister and counselors told Kenna she would never work again, and that she would be in and out of psychiatric institutions for the rest of her life. She was told by her psychiatrist that "coping" was all she could hope for. Kenna fought - she was a fighter - and today has proven those predictions wrong. Maslow's Hierarchy of Needs was a dream for her in those days; she yearned to be self-actualized. It *could* happen. And it did.

Fast forward to 2012. Kenna is self-supporting through a home based medical transcription business which she began in 1999. She has lived alone in the same rented studio suite since 2005. Her children are adults. The eldest child was given up for adoption when Kenna was 17 years old. He found her through an adoption finder's agency in Lethbridge in 2001, completing her life. Kenna therefore has three children and three grandsons. She considers herself a successful mother, having raised two children who are independent, happy, successful adults who give back to society; and a third delightful young man who lived a better life than she could have given him at the time.

The children are most important and then work, friendships and hobbies. Kenna's articles, poems, and a play have been published in numerous journals. Two books have been released, an anthology of poetry called DISCOVERY-An Anthology of Poetry, published by Authors for a Cause, and SPACEHIVE, her first young adult sci-fi novel first published by Imajin Books and now by Creativia. Both are available on Amazon.com.

She enjoys caricaturing friends and family and making her own greeting cards. Her brother gives her hints on how to play her acoustic guitar. She practices physical fitness and has a mini-gym at home in her small suite. She has several good friends. Her business is successful. She has written four novels throughout the past 25 years.

Kenna has been receiving a depot injection of Fluanxol every two to three weeks since 1991, and her mood is stable. She was last hospitalized in 1990 when she quit taking her (oral) medications at the time, and the old delusions and obsessions re-surfaced. Her psychiatrist retired in the mid-1990s and did not refer her to another psychiatrist. She sporadically obtained therapy from psychiatric nurses and finally, an RN, through a mental health clinic. Her family physician continued to prescribe Fluanxol and then Celexa as well, and she obtained depot injections through the medical clinic at which her family doctor worked. Most of the time, for the past 35 years, Kenna struggled on her own with the help of psychotropic medications and occasional therapy.

The medications and therapists, although entreated, were unable to allay underlying delusions involving control and obsessions Kenna was powerless to understand or completely resist.

These symptoms were to hound her and disrupt the lives of children, family and close friends intermittently since the illness first became apparent in 1975. But there is hope. A new psychiatrist; several resolving issues from the past; a new serendipitous antidepressant medication (Celexa), which she took for the treatment of Seasonal Affective Disorder in the winter of 2009 and repeated in the winter of 2010. Celexa apparently also treats the delusions and obsessions which had tortured her for 35 years, making them more manageable and eventually they almost disappeared.

In time, a new psychiatrist, a clever woman who figured out the significance of the Celexa, offered to take Kenna as a patient. Perhaps Kenna's delusions could have been helped or alleviated years ago? No matter, they weren't and the universe is now running as it should. Kenna has only hope for the future.

Now she is sure that this is the best year of her life and a prelude to even better times, life and love as well as joy in living.

Kenna was interviewed in November 2010 by the editor of *Grey Matters*, the newsletter of the Schizophrenia Society of Alberta. An excerpt follows.

When were you diagnosed with schizophrenia? Could you tell us a bit about that time?

"I was diagnosed in 1978 but started to show symptoms in 1975 when I was a student at the University of Alberta. I graduated with Distinction with a BA in 1975. I had wanted to go on and take a PhD but couldn't continue because of my illness. I took some more courses as a special student after I graduated, but became very ill in 1976.

"I went untreated for two or three years, unmedicated, frightened, and violent. I got into trouble with the law due to many delusions which turned into an obsession which has only recently been allayed. I have never had auditory hallucinations other than thinking I heard a radio playing Hawaiian music for a few weeks when I was in a psych unit. I used to have visual hallucinations when I was unmedicated.

"I was admitted to the forensic unit of Alberta Hospital in 1978 and was in and out of hospital for approximately one year. I worked as well as I could. My first husband had died in 1970. I had two small children, who were cared for by relatives and my brother and his wife at various times, but for most of the time I was able to care for them except when I was acutely ill. I worked as a temporary research assistant for a couple of years during the early 1980s then got a job as a secretary to the Director in a hospital setting, where I stayed for five years.

"During the early 1980s I married again and was divorced five or six years later. I continued working at the hospital setting until 1988 or 1989 then worked at the University of Alberta as an Administrative Secretary for about two years.

"I stopped taking my medication in 1990 and became ill and in trouble with the law again, same thing, a delusion that someone was trying to control me. I was again admitted to the forensic unit of Alberta Hospital. I was put on a depot injection of Fluanxol, which worked wonderfully, and I obtained long term disability from my job at the U of A for two years, although I worked most of that time at temporary clerical jobs. My children by that time were older and looked after things at home for me.

"The last time I was hospitalized was in 1990. I worked three temporary clerical jobs after that until I was hired permanently and full-time by an Oral Pathologist, for whom I worked for eight years until he retired. I then started my own medical transcription business at the suggestion of a co-worker.

"My employers all have been wonderful, almost without exception, and did make allowances for the fact that often I'd be late for work or miss days. I did try to make it up and was a good employee. But still, I had wonderful and understanding employers."

Did you take a break from work after being diagnosed?

"I was diagnosed while I was in the forensic unit of Alberta Hospital. I wasn't working at the time as I was a student at the University of Alberta trying to obtain my Master's as a special student. I took only a few classes and then had to quit. After that, during the 1980s, I took several classes at night school in Psychology at the University of Alberta, but did not finish a psychology degree.

I took various other classes since then including computer classes, a creative writing class, an art class, music lessons, Pitman shorthand, and marketing classes at NAIT fairly recently. I also took a few one-on-one classes to learn the Japanese language in 2011, but found it was too time consuming. I also go to a gym, am trying to learn to swim, and am interested in yoga and karate. I take karate lessons at Panther Gym here in Edmonton, and use their weight room as well. I've recently hired a lifestyle coach from Panther Gym to help with diet and exercise.

What inspired you to start your own company? Could you tell us a bit about your business?

"I thought when my boss retired in 1999 that I was too mature to look for another job, and I didn't feel like being in the job market again. A co-worker suggested that I start my own company. I started slowly as my boss began to work part-time, and I worked part-time for him and also started my business. I'm a medical transcriptionist and have a secure server which my son set up and maintains. I do almost exclusively digital files and have a paperless office.

"It took approximately five years to get on my feet. I worked part-time at unrelated positions such as retail and receptionist to support myself while my business was getting off the ground. It's a home-based business. I have associates I refer to who also work from home.

I'm a sole proprietorship, and make a living with the help of Old Age Security and Canada Pension Plan payments since I turned 65 and 60 respectively. I don't own a vehicle and rent a very nice little studio suite in a high rise in the Oliver district of Edmonton. I live simply. I had a listing in the Yellow Pages under "Secretarial Services" but get most of my work from word of mouth."

Could you tell us a bit about your staff?

"I don't have any staff. I work from home by myself. My associates are like me, transcriptionists who work from home, to whom I refer if I have too much work for me to do in a reasonable time frame."

Did your business ever allow you to be self-supporting?

"My business has always allowed me to be self-supporting as I supplemented it at first with part-time employment out of the home for a day or two a week. I have always been self-supporting except for a year or two when I was on disability pension from the U of A position when I became so ill in 1990. Even then I didn't get full pension because I was working part-time. Now as a senior I receive CPP and Old Age Security, which helps a lot to make up the modest income I receive as a writer and transcriptionist."

Could you tell us a bit about your hobbies?

"I'm a published writer and want eventually to make a living as a writer, but it is also a hobby. Writing poetry, drawing caricatures, making my own greeting cards for personal use, fitness such as karate and gym, walking, learning to play the acoustic guitar, studying Japanese language and culture, writing novels, short stories, and articles, I subscribed to an on-line weight loss site called Anne Collins and was active there and at church. I volunteered several hours a week."

What advice would you give other people struggling with a mental illness who want to be entrepreneurs?

"Believe in yourself, know it will be a struggle and a lot of work, be prepared to supplement your income with outside work for the first two to five years, be prepared for a lot of work, perseverance, discipline, also choose something you love and have fun with it! Get out of the house every day, go for a walk, clear your head, and - have fun! Work hard, long hours, networking with people is very important, be sure and get a business license and a good accountant, meet deadlines before they're due if possible.

"I enjoy the freedom and independence but remember nobody gives you a vacation or sick time, and you only get paid for the hours you actually work.

"This is the same advice I give to anybody else. Except maybe choose hours that would be compatible with side effects you might experience from medications, such as sedation. Let people know up front that you have a disability if you view it as a disability, but don't focus on your illness. Remember you are competing with yourself most of all, and your success depends on how hard you work and how smart you work.

"Start small, don't give up any pensions right away or part-time work, but start part-time, and have a good and realistic plan in place. Be realistic about your strengths and liabilities and work them into your business plan. Don't go over your head financially. I did that and regretted it.

"Choose something you love to do, perhaps a hobby, be innovative, think out of the box. Take some courses but get your feet wet at the same time. Don't let anyone tell you that you can't do what anyone else can do. Because you can.

When asked her philosophy of life?

"Do what you love. And do it with passion and hope. And never give up. Giving up is not an option."

Kenna penned a few verses to celebrate her freedom after being released from the psychiatric hospital in 1990. She had an empty nest, later mourned, but at the time she felt exultant to live alone without the almost constant presence of inmates and staff. She had gone for long walks alone in the grounds of the hospital when she could. Now she left her rented townhouse and moved across the street to an apartment complex where she eagerly rented a suite on the main floor. She was to stay here for the next five years.

Her daughter cross stitched a pretty card to celebrate with her. "Happy housewarming! I hope you enjoy your freedom in your very own place." Kenna still has this card. She is grateful to her son as well for his care and concern while she was acutely ill.

"A room of one's own," said Woolf. She was right.
I did not understand before.
Four spacious rooms, a window bright
And I can close the door.

A view of grass and trees outside
My very own a chair to sit
The moon at night the sky will ride
I write and see the shadows flit.

No one else cooks on my stove
Nor decorates my rooms for me
And I entertain with love
And love fine company.

A lamp, a bed, a table there
My place is fine, and slowly grows
I fill my life with love and care
And from my heart this song arose.
- Kenna McKinnon, September 9, 1990

The verses are rough. The sentiment is joy. Panther, her tuxedo cat, was to join her as her loving feline companion for a few years until he mysteriously disappeared out the patio doors one fine June morning, perhaps to catch a moving truck. Kenna met this cat, her best friend, in 1992 and they later shared another friend's charming gingerbread 100-year-old house for the next eight years.

Again, the allure of "a room of one's own" beckoned and Kenna moved to the Oliver area of downtown Edmonton where she still resides. The decades spent healing in the 1990s and during the Millennium so far have been a time of adventure and discovery, pain and occasional depression, old delusions resurfacing at times, but steady progress to a brighter future.

She has a blog at http://kenna-differentfolks.blogspot.com/. There part of her journey is chronicled, and there you may discover a living, hurting, joyful, intelligent human being who has made many mistakes. "I don't know who I am," she said once as a young woman. Kenna has finally embarked on the final joyful adventure, that of discovering who she is.

This business called schizophrenia…won't you join us on our journey of disclosure and exploration? I warn you, curious reader, it's a journey fraught with peril, heights of joy and abysses of despair.

But you may find at the other end of it that *we* are humanity and we are *you* or someone very close to you.

Kenna says, "I was diagnosed in 1978 with paranoid schizophrenia, the beginning of many years of angst and mental toil and suffering. Although I seldom struggle now, the darkness closes in on occasion."

But doesn't everyone at one time or another struggle with the "slings and arrows of outrageous fortune"? A wise man once said the majority of people "live lives of quiet desperation." If that's true, our illness has given me an appreciation of the peaceful valley beyond the rough slopes.

Are they taking the word "normal" out of the dictionary? We don't think they should. But really, the degrees of "normal" are almost infinite. Is anyone really normal? And what about the millions with disabilities? Millions of people with physical disabilities have spokespersons like Rick Hansen, Christopher Reeve or Helen Keller. Who speaks for us? We must come out of the shadows.

A man by the name of Bill MacPhee came out of the shadows. Successful, dynamic, and a businessman who owns a publishing company and spends much of his time as a speaker and entrepreneur, Kenna came across his name when she submitted an article to his magazine (SZ Magazine), and was privileged to share a couple of emails with him. Bill has schizophrenia, was hospitalized six times, attempted suicide once, spent time in three group homes. He pulled himself together, let's say, in a way that only those of us who share the same diagnosis can appreciate as superlative.

There are others. Austin Mardon has received numerous honors for his tireless work on behalf of those with mental illness. Diagnosed with schizophrenia in 1992 at the age of 30, Dr. Mardon earned his PhD in 2000 in political geography; is a writer, explorer, and researcher who lives in Edmonton, Alberta. As well, he has participated in many speaking engagements and numerous interviews throughout the province. His articles have appeared in various journals and magazines, including on-line forums.

He received his Bachelor of Arts degree from The University of Lethbridge in 1985, with a major in Geography. Mardon's website clarifies, "He went on to receive a Master's of Science degree in Geography from South Dakota State University in 1988, a Masters of Education degree from Texas A&M University in 1990, and a PhD in Geography from Greenwich University, Australia in 2000." Only the last degree was done by distance learning.

Who are *you*? What are your stories? Will you share? And what of those whose illness manifests itself more insidiously, negatively, with more dark power? Those who cannot work, cannot speak for themselves; those on the street, perhaps. There's hope.

There's a cliché. Come out of the shadows. Well, then. Come out of the shadows. We've been misunderstood, sometimes mismanaged, sometimes shunned. Find the right medication; elicit support but stand firm on your feet, contribute what you can to your own life and to society, for this is no dress rehearsal. This is your life and we're not satisfied with "coping".

As much as others with physical and cognitive disabilities have come out of the shadows, so can we. We will be joyous and self-actualized. We *will* be understood.

Austin's Story:
Austin has been ill since the fall of 1992. He had social problems all his life and had some problems since he came back from Antarctica. Austin says he may have been "really quite sick" since 1987, since his trip to Antarctica. He didn't think he was ill until 1992 when he began to think he could read people's minds, began hearing voices, thinking he was a vampire/werewolf. He would talk incoherently and wander about aimlessly. His wife in 2011 asked him if that is any different from now! Humor settles comfortably about Austin's conversations. He is a delight to hear speak.

Austin says he was living alone in a basement suite near the University of Alberta in 1992. He had a girlfriend and he asked her to marry him. She said no - and he said he "cracked." His wife chuckles, "It's a good thing I said yes." Austin agrees, "It's a good thing Catherine said yes or I would have cracked again."

Austin said he has become accustomed to the voices and visions, and the paranoia is "part of life." He takes an antipsychotic medication, Risperdal, but the symptoms haven't been completely alleviated. The symptoms have been reduced and Austin can now function but he isn't able to work full time. Austin worked for six years part-time and he presently serves on Boards and volunteers quite a bit. That's work; it's just not paid work, we agreed.

The voices usually tell Austin he's a bad person, he's going to Hell, and nobody likes him and so on. They don't tell him to hurt himself or others. Austin's voices are subdued, mostly whispers, but sometimes they break through when he is under stress. Consequently, he tries to avoid stress.

It was about three weeks before he was diagnosed and treated after becoming psychotic. He was hospitalized in November. His father knew what was happening because Austin's mother had been ill with schizophrenia. His father took him to the University of Alberta Hospital and they refused to treat Austin there. They told his father he would have to take care of Austin.

So his father left town. When Austin was admitted again later that day, the doctors didn't have any telephone numbers or anyone to refer him to, so they admitted him to the University of Alberta Hospital. This was in Edmonton in 1992.

Austin says the professionals didn't appreciate he was well educated. The doctors who know him, know better, but the professionals who don't know him assume that all people with schizophrenia are "uneducated and ignorant." Many people, especially males, become ill before they can become well educated. Austin was able to obtain three University degrees before he became ill. He feels that the professionals may have felt threatened by his higher education.

His mother and father were both very sad at the diagnosis. His sisters were angry. Austin has no brothers. He has two younger sisters. He lost most of his friends immediately. The illness impacted his life immediately.

After he had been discharged from the hospital for approximately two months, one of his close relatives told him he should get sterilized because he had schizophrenia. That was Austin's first real indication that "something was definitely different."

Austin had applied three times to be an astronaut both in the USA and Canada. He had been to the Antarctic doing research, and wanted to be a professor and do research. That all ended. What kept him going? Austin credits his Christian faith. He was born a Catholic and says his faith mostly kept him going.

Most of the people in his life disappeared except for his parents and his general practitioner. He still has the same general practitioner 20 years later.

Austin had difficulty getting the right medications until he was put on Risperdal. The doctor knew he wasn't functioning well on the previous medication he was taking. Austin credits medication as vital to recovery.

Who was most influential in Austin's recovery? He says he would "put it in stages." First his parents, especially his mother, as she had schizophrenia and she taught him how to survive with schizophrenia. Then his friends and his first wife, who left him. He was alone at that time and fell back on relying on his parents and his doctor. Then he had a circle of friends to depend on. His close friends Arthur and Leslie were important, then Catherine, his second wife, in 2005. Austin struggled for about 13 years before he met his second wife, whom he credits with much of his present stability.

Austin was on the street at one time before he became ill. He was living at the YMCA and was threatened verbally. He was afraid to go back so he "couch surfed." During that time, someone grabbed him and threw him down. He doesn't know the reason.

Austin had problems remembering to take his medication when he first became ill. He states it is very difficult and he understands why people miss taking their medications. He never intentionally missed his medications and he missed only a handful of medications over the years. But the medication improvements were of major importance.

Like Kenna, he has had many medication changes over the years. Austin still suffers from visions, paranoia and hears voices, but copes.

Austin does not have children so he feels he can speak out, but his extended and immediate family, except for his father, is ashamed of the schizophrenia. He received a very good education at the University of Lethbridge, South Dakota, and then Texas A&M, which is one of the top universities in the USA. He has been able to use his education, but Austin muses that his professors at the time didn't realize his education was going to be used in the direction in which it was used. Austin was preparing for research, life as a professor, teaching geography to either school teachers or to university students. He was trained to think well, analyze and talk in an intelligent manner as well as do paperwork and so on.

His ability to write well is still affected but the fact he was educated before he became seriously ill means he was able to finish most of his course work, except for his PhD, which he finished in 2000 at the University of Greenwich in Australia, a distance learning University. He hadn't met Catherine, his present wife, at that time. Meeting Catherine was very much a positive influence in his life. They are very congenial and Austin describes his wife as a "gentle, quiet person" who must be firm with him at times; he feels this has nothing to do with his being schizophrenic but he is sure there is a different mechanic of interacting with him as a spouse because he has schizophrenia than it would be for a "normal" person.

For example, Austin doesn't pick up on double entendres, nuances or body language. He must be directly and firmly told something and then he does it, he says, to the greatest extent he can - unless it's do the dishes! Austin laughingly says he can't do the dishes because his schizophrenia interferes with that and impairs his ability to do housework. Catherine agrees with him, of course it does!

Would the negatives outweigh the positives? On a career level, Austin's career wasn't what he thought it would be as a great scientist. He feels he could have made a great contribution intellectually to the corpus of Canadian scholarship but that didn't happen because of his illness.

Personally, he regrets not having children and not meeting his wife until they were both of mature years. Austin would have liked to have met Catherine before he became disabled so she could have known him previously. He was a bit more "feisty" back then, he says, and a lot thinner!

Austin said that people sometimes think his eccentricity is part of the schizophrenia but it's part of his personality, which Kenna finds to be true of herself as well.

People who meet him now cannot distinguish between his present life and his family culture, which includes his father being a professor and his grandfather teaching at Cambridge; his grandmother being in the first female class of PhDs in Cornell. Cornell is in New York. His father's mother was American and his father's father was British. He mother's father was British and his mother's mother was Scottish from two centuries ago in the Maritimes. Therefore, Austin is a first generation Canadian on his father's side. People tend to view that kind of intellectual upbringing and its results as abnormal, but that's not the abnormal part. The insane part of Austin's life, he notes, is in the visions and the voices he hears and so on.

Austin describes his first impression of hope. He says his visions are not all negative. Some of his visions are very ecstatic and blissful, which he states is actually more dangerous than the hallucinations that frighten him, because there's no incentive to get well or to live a life that is more boring than what the visions show him. Austin supposes the first hope came when he got married the first time in 1996, but that was like a false dawn, because she left him. A normal relationship with someone was his first hope.

Austin's first fear was when he crossed the threshold of the University of Alberta Hospital in 1992 and he realized he was being hospitalized for mental illness. He realized because of his mother's illness what that meant. He began to cry uncontrollably because he thought it was the end of his life. But it wasn't. It was just a new beginning. Sometimes the end of something is the beginning of something else.

Austin has certainly helped others. He is not part of an official one-on-one mentoring program but he does indirectly mentor people who phone him and ask him questions. He started presenting his story to 500 people at the Charles Camsell Hospital in the spring of 1993. He was asked to do that by the Schizophrenia Society of Alberta. He was volunteering then, stuffing envelopes at the Edmonton Branch of the SSA, as that was all he could do at that time.

The first advice Austin would give to someone suffering from schizophrenia today is to stay on your medications, and the second is to listen to your doctor and build a relationship with medical professionals. "You can always seek a second opinion" he says, and if you don't get along with your medical professionals it is probably a good idea to seek a new one.

However, medical professionals such as psychiatrists are very difficult to acquire. You have to "build a life," Austin says, although it may not be a "normal" life of which you may conceive, with a "white picket fence and a job." It might be different.

What's kept Austin going? The idea that his life has meaning through service to a misunderstood and mostly maligned group called schizophrenics, and on a personal level, his faith has kept him going.

Obviously, his career now is in advocacy. He still writes scientific articles but they are shorter and less detailed than they would have been otherwise. Austin reiterates that his faith has given him meaning.

He becomes disappointed when his faith community and others misunderstand him, which they have done frequently over the years. For example, his marriage was canceled three days before it was supposed to take place because Austin is schizophrenic. They had been married civilly for immigration purposes and were getting blessed when family members phoned the parish priest and advised him that Austin was ill and not taking his medication, being physically abusive towards his wife, and dangerous. It was an attempt to control Austin and separate him and his new wife.

The church sided with his family and delayed their church marriage by almost three months. They had to supply character references from approximately 25 sources, go to counseling, and endure many negative telephone calls. They did get married in 2006. Catherine became a Canadian citizen in 2011.

Catherine Mardon, Austin's wife, is a retired attorney and author. She is working on her Masters at Newman Theological College, and serves as President of the Catholic Women's League at St. Alphonsus parish. Her letter to the family on her Canadian citizenship follows:

"On January 16th, Pope Benedict gave an address for the World Day of Migrants and Refugees. He talked about the need for Christians to be welcoming to those from other lands. Globalization is leading the planet into increasing interconnectedness. He said that we all "belong to one family, migrants and the local populations that welcome them."

Those words were ringing in my ears less than a week later as I stood in a room with 81 other immigrants to Canada as we were sworn in as new Citizens.

"I never thought in my wildest dreams that I would ever become an immigrant. I grew up hearing stories about my immigrant ancestors. Dangerous sea voyages, escaping from religious persecution or famines, building colonies, and facing all manner of hardships, were not my experiences. The worst thing I dealt with was a weather delayed flight causing a 4 a.m. arrival.

"Many of the people who became citizens the same day I did worked and planned for years to come to Canada, or came here as refugees escaping horrors I can only imagine. Some came from countries that no longer exist. Until I met my future husband, I knew very little about Canada. Like many Americans, what little I thought I knew about Canada was mostly wrong.

"When Austin told me he lived in Alberta, which was north of Montana, I was dumbfounded. I didn't think anyone could live north of Montana except polar bears. Now that Alberta is my home, I'm still waiting for my first polar bear sighting.

"I may not have been fleeing a war zone, but it still wasn't easy to uproot my entire life, leave behind my friends and family, and even my dog, to come to Canada. I did it for love. I was willing to give up pretty much anything to be with my husband. Immigration can be expensive and time consuming. You must be open to having your background entirely exposed. I had to pass local, state and FBI background checks in the United States, and RCMP and CSIS checks here in Canada. I had to list every address I have lived at since I was 18 years old. I had to have my fingerprints taken twice, and pass a medical exam to make sure I wouldn't be a danger to public health. I had to be willing to answer any question the Immigration Officer asked, no matter how personal or embarrassing.

"The questions from Immigration officers were easy in comparison to the questions asked by my husband's friends and family. Why would someone living on the beach in Florida move to Edmonton in

January? Some were convinced I was a terrorist. Some believed that I must be an embezzler on the run from the law. Some even believed I was only interested in Austin's money. Those who took the time to get to know me can laugh with me about it now.

"After being sworn in as a Citizen, everyone gleefully welcomed me to Canada. The fact that I haven't stepped foot out of the country in over 5 years made the welcome kind of anti-climactic.

"I had already been welcomed warmly by the Catholic community of St. Alphonsus, especially the members of the Catholic Women's League. I've been integrated into the student body of Newman Theological College where being from someplace else is the norm rather than the exception. I've learned to deal with the metric system. The one thing that still eludes me is how to walk on the ice without damaging my dignity.

"When the process became difficult, I tried to remember other immigrants who persevered in dramatically more difficult circumstances. God asked Abraham to leave his native land, Joseph entered Egypt as slave but rose to the right hand of Pharaoh, Moses had to flee from the house of Pharaoh to be a refugee in Midian, and even Jesus spent part of his early life as a foreigner in Egypt.

"Someone asked me recently if it was all worth it. My answer was an overwhelming yes. It was a great feeling walking out of Canada Place that afternoon, knowing that no matter what happens in the future, I'll never have to be separated from my husband by a man-made border."

Austin says there is hope that there wasn't when his great-grandmother became ill with schizophrenia. Now he can have a "life." He says the medications are the first step, but there must be a purpose to take the medications. There must be meaning in life.

Austin's meaning is through advocacy and improving the lot in life of schizophrenics. This isn't easy and not simple. It's not entirely about more money for people with this illness. At times, it's simply changing some rules and making things easier for schizophrenics.

When asked about the Canadian Mental Health Act, which has recently been changed so a person can be involuntarily treated, Austin comments that he thinks it's a good improvement, and Kenna agrees. Austin comments that it is only useful for a small group of people who probably need it. Most people hopefully will come to a point where they realize they need help.

Catherine wrote the following poem about her husband on February 5, 2011:

The Man in the Mirror

I reach out my hand to touch the mirror
Just to make sure I'm real
So much of what I see eludes my touch
Reality is my Achilles' heel.

How can I know which is the voice of God
When so many voices invade?
Will I hear the voice of truth,
Or will the evil one persuade?

Sometimes I dream about the man I used to be.
I had such a future planned
But I lost that person along the way
In a way I don't understand.

Yet I still have hope of a life well lived
One step, one day at a time.
To strive for simple stability
Can make one's life sublime.

Both Mardon and Kenna have stepped out in faith, following their individual stars, in different ways. God made the world. God did not make trash. His people are guiding stars and prayer is a beacon. Find a star and God will steer.

They have survived and will continue to surprise and delight their friends and family; to astound and confound their detractors, those who would make them less than they are.

They salute the family of fellow adventurers who leap and dance on a rainbow of hope to a better life for all citizens of the world, including the percentage whom the Potter cast on a different wheel... what then, did the Potter's hand shake?

Chapter 2:
Defining Schizophrenia

"Statistics are people with the tears wiped from their eyes." –
Unknown

Throughout the world, it is estimated that approximately 51 million people suffer from schizophrenia or approximately 1 percent of the population of each country, including:

- 6 to 12 million people in China (estimate)

- 4.3 to 8.7 million people in India (estimate)

- 2.2 million people in USA

- 285,000 people in Australia

- Over 280,000 people in Canada

- Over 250,000 diagnosed cases in Britain

source: http://www.schizophrenia.com/

"I very much want to make some changes in my life and carve out a new destiny for myself now that the sentencing is over and I can move on knowing what I have to deal with," said Kenna, one of the percentage of schizophrenics who ran into trouble with the law due to persistent delusions and obsessions but no violence throughout the course of her illness.

"I'll never do it again, and to be able to determine that, I must have help. I'm seeing a new psych at FACS and am delighted. I'm going to lay on her a lot of the load to sort out, which I haven't been able to do so far. I came a long way but not far enough. It occurred to me only yesterday that I don't have to do it all myself. Nor am I alone.

"I struggled for most of my life without a lot of support, thinking I was the Lone Ranger or something. It was hard and I must say impossible to make total progress without blood, sweat and tears over a very long period of time. I don't have to do it all myself. I'm not alone.

"I'm not talking about only the psychiatrist, either, but all with whom I come into contact including the instruction I'm embarking on in the Catholic church. I've been searching for a spiritual community for so many years and didn't find it. Now I think I've found it. It'll take a year or more before I'm ready for any kind of decision but I've found a church that allows me to question and think for myself, and I'm delighted with that, too. Everything is falling into place finally and I think I just wasn't ready before.

"When the student's ready the teacher will appear. How different the last 35 years would have been had I known then what I know now! And been able to apply it."

The occurrence of schizophrenia reaches a peak between the ages of 16 and 25 years, although males commonly develop schizophrenia at an earlier age than women. It's noted that women can develop schizophrenia at around 30 years of age, as Kenna did, and again a peak is reached around 40 years of age for women. (source: www.schizophrenia.com) Children below the age of 10 and older adults rarely develop schizophrenia for the first time ("first break" psychosis), although it has been known to happen.

What is schizophrenia?

Schizophrenia is a serious mental illness characterized by hallucinations and delusions as well as disorganized speech and odd behaviors ("positive" symptoms). Negative symptoms, on the other hand, include lack of motivation, limited thought and speech, and a relative lack of emotional expression.

Schizophrenia must be diagnosed by a trained health professional, who considers "groupings" of characteristic symptoms much as you might identify a constellation of stars on a clear night. (source: http://www.mentalhealth.net/) The DSM (Diagnostic and Statistical Manual) is a manual which provides health care professionals with the criteria necessary for a correct diagnosis. Symptoms must be present from a minimum of one to six months for a diagnosis of schizophrenia to be made.

What isn't it? It isn't multiple personality disorder (associative identify disorder). Sybil didn't have schizophrenia, nor did Eve. This is a common misapprehension, perhaps brought about by the term "split personality" often connected with schizophrenia. Schizophrenia means in Greek "split mind". The previous name for this serious mental illness was "dementia praecox".

Schizophrenia has been around probably for as long as Eve first heard a talking snake or as long as our forebears came out of the trees to gather on the savanna and noticed that one of their members talked to gods.

A note of interest, anthropology classes have taught their students on occasion that those individuals who experienced hallucinations and "out of body" experiences were sometimes ejected from the tribe but frequently were deemed to be special spiritually as they could talk to gods and see visions. They were sometimes given positions of prestige by their group, such as "prophet" or "medicine man."

There are four main types of schizophrenia but symptoms in the same individual can change over time. Simple (undifferentiated) and disorganized (formerly called hebephrenic) schizophrenia usually begins during late adolescence. These patients appear apathetic or perhaps silly, and tend to withdraw from normal associations with others.

Catatonic schizophrenia usually appears later in life and may be a result of emotional trauma. The catatonic schizophrenic will remain in the same position for hours at a time and may refuse to bathe, eat or talk.

People with paranoid schizophrenia tend to experience auditory hallucinations (voices talking to them that only they can hear) or other hallucinations such as angels or other figures or objects that no one else can see, delusions such as intense suspicion and paranoia including odd religious beliefs, delusions of grandeur, or feelings of persecution. They may become violent but the majority of schizophrenics are not a danger to others. They tend to be of normal or higher intelligence.

The incidence of suicide or early death in schizophrenia is estimated to be close to 10 percent of all schizophrenics (source: www.schizophrenia.com)

Kenna went through the mid and late 1970s suffering from schizophrenia and depression, which was originally diagnosed as schizoaffective disorder. She was given various diagnoses in those years, including manic-depressive (bipolar), schizoaffective, paranoid schizophrenia, and personality disorder. This resulted in delay of appropriate treatment.

In the first instance, she was given heavy doses of oral major tranquilizers, early antidepressant medications, as well as a pill to counteract the Parkinsonian- type symptoms (tremors and rigidity of face and limbs) that were side effects of those early medications.

Treatment also consisted of lengthy stays in psychiatric hospitals (up to six months or a year) and consultations with a variety of therapists including nurses, social workers, psychologists and psychiatrists, all of whom expressed a "guarded" prognosis.

Kenna was told she would never work again and that she would be in and out of psychiatric hospitals for the rest of her life. Her parents and family seemed devastated and her parents had limited understanding of what had happened to their eldest daughter, believing that she was "bad". Friends, neighbors and co-workers made cruel jokes and comments, and Kenna suspects her children were subject to discrimination. She sold her house and moved to a different area of town after a couple of years. Her brother's wife quit her job to look after the children until Kenna was on her feet again in the early 1980s. A cousin of her former husband also took the children for a year.

Due to her late husband's life insurance benefits, Kenna had some financial means and was not forced to consider AISH or another subsidy or pension. She worked as much as she could. Her dreams of an academic career at University were dashed. She worried about her children and her behavior became increasingly narcissistic and disorganized. She began to smoke and abused alcohol as a means of "treating" her symptoms. She was suicidal.

Shortly after she married a second time in the early 1980s she underwent ECT (electroconvulsive therapy) for six weeks to treat suicidal depression. Her second marriage ended in divorce in 1987. Her children lived with her intermittently throughout this time, and most of the 1980s until they left home independently in the 1990s. Kenna is proud of her children's progress and that they have grown to be fine adults without substance abuse issues or other symptoms of mental illness.

In 1990 Kenna was working at the University of Alberta when she quit taking her medications, as she felt she was coping well and could cope without it. Within a short space of time there was a relapse of delusions and other positive symptoms. Trouble with the law followed and a period of disability from work which was covered by disability insurance. Kenna continued to work as well as she could at least part-time.

Two years later the disability payments were stopped and she continued to work for the next eight years for an oral pathologist until his retirement in 1999, when she began her own home based medical transcription business. Kenna is delighted to buy a bus pass for $13 a month rather than $84, and the other benefits seniors enjoy. Life is getting better and she doesn't anticipate another hospitalization, although recent challenges in 2009 brought her almost to her knees one more time. "Never give up" she says cheerfully, and writes and advocates for schizophrenia and those less fortunate.

Medications have improved tremendously in the 37 years since she first became ill, and therapists no longer "present reality" in the form of negativity the way they did when Kenna was first diagnosed. She is 68 years old and has had schizophrenia since she was a relatively young woman of 31. In many ways, she feels that 35 years have been lost. But there are no regrets. Her glass is filled to overflowing at this time of her life, and it has always been half full, not half empty; she has always been a fighter. These are Kenna's thoughts in the present decade, in the year 2012. She is determined to make it work this time.

At one time women who experienced difficult menopausal symptoms were sometimes declared mentally ill and locked away in a psychiatric institution for the rest of their lives. Kenna personally talked to a neighbor at one time whose mother was treated in this manner. She met her friend's mother, a pleasant woman who appeared not bitter about the long wasted years of her middle age, although this woman's other daughter was soured by the experience and blamed her mother.

People were sometimes locked in attics before the advent of institutions. Literature is replete with these horror stories (see Jane Eyre, for example). Jails are and were full of mentally ill individuals. There is little provision in court for those suffering from delusions or violent behavior because of mental illness.

The stigma was devastating. Cruel jokes and practical jokes were perpetrated on the children and family of the ill as well as on the mentally ill themselves. Jobs were denied. Marriages and families were rent apart. It was all very hush-hush.

Even today few people outside the community know anything positive about schizophrenia but only the horror stories they read in the media. Violence to others is so rare that it warrants a headline.

Schizophrenia is the unknown, the unpredictable, the dangerous. This is a common mindset and the mindset of even some in the legal profession, although police officers are increasingly being trained in the observation and handling of mentally ill people. More compassion and experience by the police has become apparent.

Mental illness is coming out of the closet. Mentors are available. Organizations such as the Schizophrenia Society of Alberta (SSA) offer speakers with presentations about the illness to interested groups at a nominal fee, support for families and members who have the illness, written material, a library full of books and DVDs that will educate and help, and mentoring for those who wish to be matched one-on-one with a more successful member of the SSA community. This latter is an interesting concept, recent in terms of Kenna's experience, and valuable she thinks.

http://www.Dictionary.com/ gives the definition of "mentor" as "a wise or trusted counselor or teacher," or "an influential senior sponsor or supporter." According to *Wikipedia*, the roots of the practice of mentoring are "lost in antiquity. The word itself was inspired by the character of Mentor in Homer's Odyssey." Wikipedia goes on to state that, "A study of mentoring techniques most commonly used in business was published in 1995 under the title *Working Wisdom*."

She was delighted to read and hear of Bill MacPhee and to meet Austin Mardon, both advocates for those suffering from mental illness, and would be thrilled to meet others like them. "I would be happy to be a role model myself, in what little and limited capacity I can," she says. "Two members of my family other than I have been diagnosed with schizophrenia. They are NOT the children I raised by myself with the invaluable assistance of my brother and his wonderful wife, as well as my first husband's cousin," she continues. "But there does seem to be a strong genetic component in my family, perhaps stemming from ancestors in Scotland long ago, as my maternal grandfather's history is not known."

Her emotions were for most of her adult life locked away in a maelstrom of confusion, anger and fear. She compartmentalized her feelings on the advice of a therapist she saw in the late 1960s, several years *before* her first breakdown. "The craft I sailed so bravely after my first husband died in 1971 was leaking by the time I met my nemesis in 1975," Kenna says, "My role models were pirates and villains gleaned from books, movies, and songs."

She didn't know any better than to be an island in the middle of the perfect storm, battered on all sides, hurting her friends and family and herself most of all — what role models were there for her in those days, the 1970s to the 1990s, other than therapists who told her she would never work again?

"I overlooked some individuals who could and would have helped," Kenna muses. "I felt I wasn't worthy of those who would befriend me positively, perhaps those who had been there before (I didn't know; will never know). I was a rock. I was an island."

"For there *have* been mentors in my life. I wouldn't be so hasty anymore to refuse guidance. I remember those who tried to help me, and they sometimes took strange guises as well; some I interpreted as my enemies," Kenna confides. "We need mentors and role models. I am very grateful for the mentors in my life."

Mardon states that simply by living well and being open about the mental illness is advocacy. He as well as Bill MacPhee are role models for many who are grateful to know of their struggles and successes. Where are the rest? We need a Christopher Reeves of schizophrenia; a Terry Fox of mental illness.

The mentally ill are often marginalized and given caregivers rather than role models. That is merely 20th Century misinformation and disparagement! Medication is the key but not the whole answer. Take your meds. Find a star to guide you. Let's help one another.

It's estimated that if research on mental illness were given appropriate funding as other illnesses have access to, a cure for schizophrenia could be found within 10 years. In 2001, there were 15 new medications for treatment. "Talking therapy" such as CBT (cognitive behavioral therapy) shows great promise.

Magazines such as Magpie Press's *SZ Magazine* are geared specifically towards educating members and the public about this debilitating disease. Mental illness is slowly becoming more accepted and acknowledged, and we predict that in the future this will skyrocket. Mental illness will be the poster child of tomorrow.

Office burnout, economic stress, post-traumatic syndrome in returning soldiers, the abuse of drugs and alcohol, particularly in the young who seem most vulnerable to the incidence of "first break," will spawn new generations of those who experience "first break" episodes of psychosis. They will need treatment, and they will be more open and accepting and vocal for recognition and cure. No longer will doctors and our families lock us away into institutions for the rest of our lives, nor will they relegate us to the fringes of society. We will be heard!

New theories of the causes of schizophrenia are being researched. No longer do doctors talk exclusively of genetic links or schizophrenia being "formed in the womb" or genetically inherited. A promising theory takes into account biology or heredity as well as early childhood experiences, ethnicity, culture and traumatic experiences which may trigger the incidence of the disease. It's called the Biopsychosocial Theory.

It may even make possible the prevention of schizophrenia.

Biopsychosocial Theory

The bio-psycho-social model of illness (BPT) was postulated in an article published 1977 in *Science* by psychiatrist Dr. George L. Engel, who described the biological, psychological and social interactions which could produce a disease or illness such as schizophrenia. This contrasts with the old "mechanical" model which thinks of our brain as being "hard wired" from birth, or even in the womb.

Acceptance of the new model varies across practitioners and even cultures (source: http://www.wikipedia.org/) but it is increasingly accepted today, although little understood by the public, media, and organizations such as insurance companies, who apparently confuse BPT with psychosomatic illness or "malingering". This is an erroneous assumption and needs more education and understanding of the complex interactions between environment and genes, or "nature and nurture."

Interestingly, thousands of years before Dr. Engel's introduction of the theory in 1977, evidence of application of this theory was found in ancient Asia (2600 BC) and Greece (500 BC). (source: http://www.wikipedia.org/) Followers of Hippocrates perhaps take note. The venerable Greek doctor may have made use of this theory back then when temple goddesses perhaps were seeing visions and taking drugs, or young premature Don Quixote and Oedipus tilted at the Sphinx.

Let's be up-to-date, folks, but use our intelligence, as mankind has since history began. King Lear may not have gone mad had it not been for his daughters' treatment of him and the division of his kingdom, and he may not have recovered had it not been for Cordelia...there are secrets known by philosophers and artists that are just making their way into science.

Secrets known to science are just making their way into the general consciousness of the public today. Does it take a rocket mechanic to consider the impact of environment on a malleable young mind, particularly a mind with a genetic predisposition? This is not to blame upbringing alone as genetics also plays a major role. Truth is not black and white as we believed in the first blush of our understanding.

Chemical Imbalance

Experts don't know why the psychotropic medications work. There are theories, and they seem to us to be sound, that the brain works through chemical interactions across synaptic gaps (neurotransmitters). The antipsychotic medications block the neurotransmitter dopamine and antidepressants will inhibit the uptake of serotonin and norepinephrine (source: http://allpsych.com/); they change a chemical imbalance and that results almost magically in the righting of a tilted mind.

There were approximately 15 or more new psychotropic medications under development in the last eight years (source: http://www.schizophrenia.com/), all of which work to block or enhance neurotransmitters in the brain to correct a chemical imbalance. It seems to make sense because they work.

Virus in the Womb

BBC News first reported the discovery of a relationship between the influenza virus in the first trimester of life in the womb and later schizophrenia (reported August 2004). This study needed follow-up confirmation but was the first to study individual responses to the flu virus rather than the study of populations. Researchers had analyzed stored blood samples of mothers of patients with schizophrenia to determine the presence of flu antibodies from birth.

The research was led by New York's Columbia University and was published in *Archives of General Psychiatry*. They estimate that as much as 14 percent of schizophrenia cases may be linked to exposure to the flu virus in the womb. (source: http://news.bbc.co.uk/)

Research reported in September 2010 indicates that birth trauma or complications within the womb, maternal flu, and winter birth is a risk factor for schizophrenia and bipolar illness possibly because of the increased likelihood of viruses during the winter. (source: http://www.mentalhealthchannel.net/)

Role of Genetics

In 2009, it was reported by "an international team of researchers" that a rare mutation on a human chromosome increased by 8x the risk of schizophrenia in individuals that had this double gene. (source: http://www.physorg.com/) Deletions on certain chromosomes are also a potent risk factor for schizophrenia. Further study needs to be done, but this research indicates that risk factors for schizophrenia can be higher for certain individuals than in the general population.

No genetic tests are currently available but rather extensive re-search has been done on the relationship between genetics and schizophrenia in studies with close family members and identical twin studies. (source: http://www.schizophrenia.com/)

It's noted that schizophrenia in identical twins is less than 60 percent, which indicates that "schizophrenia is not entirely a genetic disease." (source: www.schizophrenia.com) Interestingly, they go on to state that "The current belief is that there are several genes that contribute to susceptibility or pathology of schizophrenia, but *none exhibit full responsibility for the disease...* " (our italics) "It is believed that schizophrenia is much like diabetes, which is caused by a number of genetic and environmental factors. Research also increasingly suggests that - like diabetes - many cases of schizophrenia may be preventable."

Preventable? Fascinating... we'll discuss this later, though we've touched on that earlier, when we hinted at factors responsible for developing schizophrenia. Although the genetic predisposition may be there, environmental and social factors may be supportive of the individual and thus she will not develop the illness. Or the mother may take preventive measures while the child is in the womb and not develop the virus, or perhaps not take the over-the-counter medication that may be responsible.

In the past, those who had schizophrenia have often been encouraged not to have children, even by knowledgeable and otherwise compassionate physicians who have suggested routine sterilization of those adults before they become fathers or mothers ("Eugenics" - see below).

This isn't new. Inmates of psychiatric institutes and hospitals for the mentally challenged were routinely sterilized without their knowledge in the first half of the twentieth century (source: www.wikipedia.org) in the so-called "enlightened" countries of North America and Europe. "About 2,832 adults and children were sterilized in Alberta, Canada between the passing of the Sexual Sterilization Act in 1928 and its repeal in 1972." There was a recent class action suit in Canada concerning this horrific policy.

"After a survivor won a $1 million lawsuit in 1996, the 700 remaining survivors joined a $700 million class action lawsuit… the Alberta legislature limited the compensation to a maximum of $150,000 per victim." (source: http://www.faqs.org/health/topics/45/Eugenics)

"DNA is Not Destiny." (source: http://www.geneimprint.com/)

There may be ways to change our genes through diet, habits, environment and health. An intriguing thought and one worth pursuing. Is it possible to change our genes to benefit our future descendants? The article by Ethan Waters appears to challenge old notions of "hard wiring" and "genetic destiny."

We will also touch on the topic of fundamentalists and the concept of "God's punishment" for "sins" of the individual who suffers or his parents or ancestors. This would seem after a bit of thought to support the concept of genetic predetermination, or perhaps a wild attempt at branding those who are different in some way as "my way or the highway"…or a fear of the unknown, perhaps… or a precursor to eugenics? Eugenics means in Greek "good in birth" and was first coined by Francis Galton in 1883. (source: http://www.faqs.org/health/topics/45/Eugenics.html)

It's noted that the Roman Catholic Church *opposed* sterilization on "religious grounds" during the time that eugenics was practiced in North America and Europe.

One more area of fascinating research is developed in the book by Dr. Norman Doidge, *The Brain that Changes Itself,* which proposes that we *can* change our brains. This is not easy, but we are not "hard wired," says Dr. Doidge. He proposes that the "neuroplasticity" (or cortical re-mapping) of the brain enables our brains to change physically in response to experience. The brain can heal or change itself. His research is well documented in the book and we would recommend it for anyone really interested in changing a situation long thought to be exclusively genetic or traumatic and intractable. It is not.

Kenna was once invited by a well-meaning RN to attend a session on management of clients with schizophrenia. The course was attended by half a roomful of interested people who seemed to be primarily caregivers. The focus of the course seemed to be on caregiving. Although this course was presented approximately 20 years ago, Kenna's chagrin remains that the two nurses who presented the course appeared to have "knowledge" only of the caregiving role of the family and friends and didn't support the autonomy, the potential career paths, the happiness or the self determination of the individual who had been diagnosed with this illness, nor were the individual's wishes taken into consideration.

Kenna felt she was the "token patient" as the coordinator of the course had asked her to attend this meeting and identify herself as someone who had schizophrenia. The RN looked at her expectantly at the "right" time.

Later Kenna answered a few innocuous questions from the caregivers and one informed her she was impressed with the courage necessary to admit to such an illness in front of strangers. Kenna, ill and confused, felt she again had been manipulated.

Whether this is true or not is a moot point as someone who had been diagnosed with paranoid schizophrenia certainly should have been treated more sensitively by "therapists" familiar with the illness. This is an example, however, of caregivers being taught the "hard wired" theory which was the medical model at the time.

The RNs who presented the course have long since moved on although the course was offered for a few more years at a community college.

Neuroplasticity? Yes, with great difficulty but it is possible, and in those days it wasn't even thought the brain could be changed.

What is schizophrenia? Can we change the pathways in our brain? How do the medications work? Does cognitive behavioral therapy really work? And why is society so slow in recognizing that we are victims and have been victims often since early in our childhoods?

Neuroplasticity? Kenna proved it. It was necessary to fight. How unpopular Kenna was at times, how little support she got from family and friends, and therapists. As late as 2003 a psychiatric nurse to whom

Kenna was assigned as a patient at a Government of Alberta mental health clinic told her that she would have to live with the delusions and obsessions. There was no help available. She was told she had "boundary problems."

She was given an appointment to see the therapist eight months down the road; when she asked for help she was told by the therapist that the therapist treated only individuals who needed minimal assistance.

Kenna's psychiatrist had retired many years earlier and referred her to her family physician and the mental health clinic. Efforts to find help failed.

Perhaps she was not ready? That's possible, she concedes. When the student is ready the teacher will appear.

The docile, the acquiescent sufferers, were encouraged. Fighters, the feisty ones who made trouble for the system, were discouraged and put down at that time, 35 years ago, 20 years ago, 5 years ago. Now.

When the charity for handicapped people (the blind) with whom Kenna had volunteered so capably since 2001 discovered from a cursory look at a blog that Kenna was charged with an offense, they withdrew all support from her and refused further contact.

The elderly visually challenged friend with whom Kenna had volunteered as a "friendly visitor" remains to this day a dear friend. The charity ignored Kenna's infrequent attempts at explanation. Kenna withdrew voluntarily when it became apparent the charity had misunderstood and overreacted to her situation, long before there was evidence of any wrongdoing.

Such misunderstanding and judgment continued throughout her adult life since the schizophrenia first made itself evident in 1975. There is a gross misunderstanding by most of society of what is entailed by the delusions, the obsessions, and what strength of character was needed to recover and admit publicly to the disability. But schizophrenia need not be a handicap.

Kenna's life went on, and is better for her experiences, she feels, than if she had not become ill nor met her nemesis in 1975.

Will the meek inherit the earth? Not in her experience. But there's room for compromise. If one can think clearly, there's room to fight for self-respect and dignity. There's room to fight the ignorance that abounds in society and the cruelty of it all. And fight it she did. Kenna changed her brain. Not enough; as in 2009 she contacted the old acquaintance first met in 1974 in University and was charged with criminal harassment. She wanted help and she got it. "I'm in trouble with the law. And I'm schizophrenic. Why didn't I get the treatment I sought in previous years for the delusions and obsessions which tortured me? I found help only recently, at the Forensic Services to which I was referred at my sentencing in January."

Thus Kenna, a nonviolent offender, started the new year with renewed hope and determination to get the help she found through the courts. She is also very grateful for the support of friends and family, her children, her family doctors and the FACS workers and psychiatrist who eventually assessed her, her lawyer, and for the encouragement of the Schizophrenia Society of Alberta.

The Mental Health Act was changed somewhat in January 2010 to include revisions to involuntary admissions and the addition of Community Treatment Orders, which are involuntary orders to individuals to obtain treatment in the community if further treatment is deemed necessary after discharge from a psychiatric institution.

Kenna says, "In my opinion, this is a good thing to ensure that people at risk of further harm don't fall between the cracks, as has been the case in previous years…"

Follow-up treatment in the community by skilled mental health care provisioners and compliance with medications is critical to prevent relapse and the use of already overtaxed jails, which are pretty obviously not appropriate places for a person with mental illness. Thankfully, community service orders are commonly given in lieu of jail time or fines for those whose finances are limited.

Often those with mental illness receive advice or suggestions from family members or acquaintances which are not sound and based on faulty or thoughtless evidence.

"So many people thought they knew better than I about the machinations of the illness within me," says Kenna. "A family member suggested I take massive doses of vitamins at one time, something she'd read about. I read a book once called *I Never Promised You a Rose Garden* which I thought was excellent, although it's fiction. I mentioned it to a family member, who thought instead a book about depression was more appropriate for me. I wasn't depressed. I was paranoid and schizophrenic.

"People in positions of trust offered dubious advice and suggestions in the late 1970s and 1980s when I first became ill," Kenna says. "At one time, a minister I told me 'could never work again, of course.' I was told by a social worker you don't *have* schizophrenia, you *are* schizophrenic. The same social worker sadly shook his head in 1978 and said, 'I'm sorry to hear that' when I told him my diagnosis."

Professional training and treatments have leapt into the more enlightened 21st Century but the stigma is still embraced by many who should know better. Few therapists now would agree with Kenna's psychiatrist in the mid-1980s, who told her she could expect no more than to "cope" when she felt she was on a plateau. She told him her goal was to be self-actualized, a term she'd studied in university. "He told me I should be satisfied with coping," she laughs and continues, "I was told by staff in a psychiatric hospital that I would be in and out of mental hospitals for the rest of my life. At that time, mental health professionals thought they were doing a service to a client by presenting 'reality.' Things have changed a lot since then."

Health care professionals are much more positive; much more knowledgeable; much more helpful; and medications have improved tremendously.

"I haven't been hospitalized since 1990, when I stopped taking my medication for a couple of months just prior to that, a very big mistake. I've faithfully taken a depot injection every two to three weeks since that time," Kenna says, "never missing an injection. But I fell between the cracks. My psychiatrist retired and referred me to a mental health community agency which eventually did not assist me. I found myself floundering by April 2009 and suffering with longstanding delusions and obsessions; in trouble both emotionally and legally. Fortunately, I received some of the help I needed without the need for hospitalization, partially through the same community mental health agency with a new therapist and new restructuring, partially through more formal sources." Finally, inevitably, through legal channels, but without the need for a jail sentence.

"I've been helped by this new change in the Mental Health Act," she says, "No one likes to be involuntarily treated. However, the nature of our illness is delusion and often fraught with denial and noncompliance; if I needed help and were unable to help myself I would welcome now what would have been viewed as invasive at one time."

We've found acceptance and understanding from our fellows. It wasn't until she found others with the same diagnosis or similar (bipolar illness can be similar in its symptoms in many ways to schizophrenia), that in the last part of the winter of 2011 Kenna at last began to feel the non-judgmental acceptance and support that should be everyone's birthright.

This involved a caring and understanding family doctor and LPN at her medical clinic, a resource she had ignored; nurses, assistants and psychiatrists at the Forensic Assessment and Community Services (FACS), a competent and compassionate lawyer, supportive friend and family. This is our birthright.

Sticks and stones can break our bones, but names *can* hurt us. Grievously. There were those who hurt us. Friends of family members who should know better. How quick to kick those who are down, how quick to accuse and judge. Those of us who suffer know all too well the cruelty of humanity toward those who are different. That's why so many hide their illness and refuse to speak of it. That's why mental illness remains a pariah even today, in an otherwise enlightened age.

And that's why we speak out here.

It must be emphasized here that we don't blame our families nor our parents for our schizophrenia. It seems it was inevitable. Perhaps given different circumstances the prognosis may have been better - or worse. Who can tell? These are all theories.

Many have survived worse childhoods and come out of it perhaps with other problems or stronger for it, or more compassionate, or more bitter. No parent is perfect and that's why we enjoy being grandparents so much - we've learned our lessons and can relive the opportunity to rectify mistakes made with our own children.

Only those who have children of their own can appreciate the challenges and joys of parenthood, and can appreciate the fact that we make many mistakes yet love unconditionally. Mistakes that damage young spirits may be irreparable. But the resiliency of children and the resiliency of the human spirit are remarkable.

Please don't blame mom and dad. Don't blame your friends. Don't blame your upbringing. Don't even blame the genes. Let's just get on with it. It's here. Others might have crippling arthritis, diabetes, heart disease, lupus, cancer, MS…we have a mental disability.

"There were times in my childhood I thought I'd been left by aliens," laughs Kenna. "I was waiting for them to come and take me back." Childhood? Was the genesis of the illness coiled in her DNA even back then, coiled in her brain and heart, not recognized nor discovered until she was in her early 30s?

Or did it incubate then, a shy and repressed child, bullied at school, brighter than her peers at first and later struggling emotionally to make it through high school with grades that would later qualify her to attend university as a regular student at the age of 26.

Her husband had died, leaving an insurance policy that was to last until her second marriage and divorce in 1987.

Kenna fulfilled a lifelong dream of attending University. In her last semester, she floundered with mental illness and almost fell to her knees with the agony of missed opportunities, shattered relationships, and separation from her children and family for at least a time.

The gene is crafty, perhaps lurking in Kenna's extended family, perhaps stemming from Scotland long ago with a mysterious maternal or paternal ancestor. The schizophrenia was a surprise, not expected, not encountered in the family before Kenna's first major breakdown in 1975 and ultimately the diagnosis, and delayed help, in 1978.

The longer one delays treatment after the "first break" the more difficult the schizophrenia is to treat, and the more guarded the prognosis. Kenna is fortunate. She fought and won over odds that send others to the street or repeatedly in and out of mental institutions for the rest of their lives.

Yes, it was hard. It's a hard and insidious disease that lays many a good man and woman low as do the sister mental illnesses like bipolar.

There were those who could have helped but the ship Kenna sailed was a solitary one. She had learned to expect and accept no help and that her illness was a sign of weakness. Gazing at the evil reflected back at her from a mental mirror, she was to flounder with limited degrees of success for the next 35 years.

Chapter 3:
Treating Schizophrenia

"In nothing do men more nearly approach the gods than in giving health to men". - Cicero
[*Author's note: **or women!**]

Medications are the offensive tackles in our line of scrimmage. The relapse rate of the illness amongst those who fail to take their medications has been estimated at 80 percent within 2 years. (source: www.schizophrenia.com)

"Estimates of noncompliance range between 4% and 92% with average from 30 to 35 percent" (Feuertein et al., 1986).

Noncompliance is the most common cause of relapse.

Reasons given for noncompliance are usually side-effects such as weight gain or sedation, the cost of drugs, or poor comprehension by the patient. Better community services and education are vital for those who are not in a formal setting. (source: Rekha Roy, Masroor Jahan, Sushma Kumari, and Prashant Kumar Chakraborty, Ranchi Institute of Neuro-Psychiatry and Allied Sciences, Ranchi.)

Depot injections, a needle filled with psychotropic medication that lasts from two to three weeks, such as Kenna takes, are preferable for those with compliance issues or those who don't tolerate oral drugs well. Side effects are less intrusive and less frequent and may dissipate with time. The medications need be injected only once every 2 - 3 weeks, thus eliminating the need to remember to take your pills daily, or the increased side effects that often accompany the oral drugs.

Research is exciting and promises new and more effective medications within a few years with fewer side effects.

Today the medications are generations removed from the major tranquilizers and old Tricyclic antidepressants Kenna took in the late 1970s and 1980s. She is grateful for research and looks forward to more funding for mental health research so a cure for schizophrenia might be found.

For example, on February 3, 2011 findings were published in the online issue of the journal *Nature* that "In a major advance for schizophrenia research, an international team of scientists, led by Jonathan Sebat, PhD, assistant professor of psychiatry and cellular and molecular medicine at the University of California, San Diego School of Medicine, has identified a gene mutation strongly linked to the brain disorder – and a signaling pathway that may be treatable with existing compounds...the gene identified by the researchers is an especially attractive target for drug development [for schizophrenia]. In some ways, this is the kind of gene that the pharmaceutical industry has been waiting for, said Sebat, who is also chief of the Beyster Center for Molecular Genomics of Neuropsychiatric Diseases and a member of the Institute for Genomic Medicine, both at UC San Diego." (source: http://www.psypost.org/)

Cognitive Behavioral Therapy (CBT) promises a therapeutic approach to managing symptoms such as delusions, hallucinations and negative symptoms such as apathy and lack of motivation, by addressing the behavior in order to change thoughts and feelings that may precipitate the symptoms or the area from which they arise.

In January 2011 Kenna attended a presentation sponsored by the Schizophrenia Association of Alberta (SSA) on the use of CBT for control of symptoms. The meeting was attended by health care professionals, caregivers, staff and members of the SSA. A moderately high amount of interest was shown for the presentation and it sparked a desire in us to learn more about this popular form of therapy. CBT is a talking therapy used in conjunction with pharmacology (psychotropic drugs) to treat the long-term effects of schizophrenia. "The CBT treatment cannot treat people with schizophrenia completely. However, the psychotic episodes may be reduced and hospitalization terms may also be reduced through use of CBT and drugs." (source: http://www.ehow.com/how_5054587_treat-schizophrenia-cbt.html).

This therapy was used in the United Kingdom for decades before acceptance in the United States. Reasons for this have been cited as the prevalence of biology-based medicine in the United States. In Canada, CBT appears now to have become widely accepted amongst therapists. Family physicians are offered courses such as the Continuing Medical Education courses featured in the B.C. Medical Journal in January/February 2011. They are advised that "Medical cognitive behavioral therapy enables you to provide more effective psychological care within your standard-length family practice appointments. In 2011, CBT Canada is offering 12 Mainpro-C accredited medical CBT workshops". (source: http://www.bcmj.org/cme/listings)

We found a study, however, reported in the online journal *Psychological Medicine* in which Professor Keith Laws, at the University's School of Psychology was one of the lead authors on a paper entitled: *Cognitive behavioural therapy for major psychiatric disorder: does it really work?"*

The authors "review the use of CBT in schizophrenia, bipolar disorder and major depression" and come to the conclusion that "cognitive therapy is of no value in schizophrenia... The results of the review suggest that not only is CBT **ineffective** in treating schizophrenia and in preventing relapse, it is also ineffective in preventing relapses in bipolar disorder." (source: http://www.physorg.com/news165230967.html) The jury is out.

Other treatments include group dynamics or group therapy, long used in psychiatric hospitals and outpatient groups; regression therapy under hypnosis; psychotherapy and psychoanalysis; and other one-on-one or group attempts at treatment. These should always be used in conjunction with medication under the supervision of a doctor but can certainly augment the time-tested strategy of drugs combined with "talk" therapy.

Alternative treatments include dietary supplements which "have proven to have dramatic effects on the symptoms of schizophrenia." You are cautioned that these should be used only under the close supervision of a doctor and in conjunction with an antipsychotic and/or antidepressant (for those with schizoaffective disorder or concomitant depression). (source: http://www.epigee.org/mental_-health/schizophrenia_treatment.html)

- **Glycine Supplements**: Glycine, an amino acid, is shown to help alleviate negative symptoms in schizophrenics by up to 24%.

- **Omega-3 Fatty Acids**: Found in fish oils, Omega-3 fatty acids high in EPA can help to reduce positive and negative symptoms associated with schizophrenia.

- **Antioxidants**: The antioxidants Vitamin E, Vitamin C, and Alpha Lipoic Acid show a 5 to 10% improvement in symptoms of the disorder.

Caregiving:

This section on treatment wouldn't be complete without a discussion of the caregivers who often form such an important piece of the mosaic. We're social creatures and our physical, mental, emotional and spiritual health depends on community. Also, those in the acute or chronic stages of the disease often can't care completely for themselves.

Ongoing financial assistance may be needed in the form of a pension such as AISH (Assured Income for the Severely Handicapped), CPP or perhaps a private pension. Forms need to be filled out, calls made; perhaps the individual doesn't have a vehicle and needs someone to drive her to appointments and doctors' visits; perhaps she needs help with household chores and tasks of daily living; perhaps she doesn't understand the need for compliance with medications; perhaps she needs her medications given to her. Group homes provide this sort of support. Many of us live independently. But for most of us, at one time or another, we've needed a caregiver.

The caregiver should allow us to be as independent as possible and live as "normal" a life as possible, but be cognizant of the presence of symptoms when they arise. Kenna and Austin depend on friends and family to recognize when something's wrong and to steer us gently back to center. Aging parents, a sibling or spouse, children or professional caregivers are often cast in the role of caregiver.

A little humor goes a long way. At those times, you may know us better than we know ourselves. You sometimes are required to be our mirror or our sounding board. Like a clanging gong or a cymbal, we are nothing without love.

Chapter 4:
The Role of Environment in Schizophrenia

"Nobody can be uncheery with a balloon." - A.A. Milne

If you're happy and you know it, clap your hands (clap clap)
If you're happy and you know it, clap your hands (clap clap)
If you're happy and you know it, then your face will surely show it
If you're happy and you know it, clap your hands. (clap clap)

I wasn't a happy child. I was loved, but abused from outside the family and carried heavy responsibilities for my young age; lack of good friends; bullying in school; loneliness and... *wait!!!* Was it really that way? NO!!

I grew up on a small farm in northeastern British Columbia. It was a *great* place to grow up! I remember spending quadrillions of hours in solitary play or with my siblings. I rode my favorite pony to school. We had dogs and cats and pigs and chickens and cows... a creek running through gentle knolls and grassy places; trees flashing silver green in the summer breezes; snow tunnels and ice skating in the winter; the boys played rink hockey and made their own bows and arrows...occasionally a favorite cousin or a friend from town would stay with us.

I sometimes visited with my aunt and uncle in Pouce Coupe and my cousins, or with friends in Rolla, our nearest hamlet, which boasted a small grocery store, a confectionary at one time, a post office and a very large old hotel and "beer parlor" where one of my uncles would disappear for hours at a time.

There were picnics at the end of every school year, and Christmas concerts every year with a real, live Santa Claus.

For a special treat my mother would sit my sister and me down and share with us a cup of hot tea loaded with lots of milk and sugar when dad and my brothers were gone. My faithful little sister adored me and I told her bedtime stories every night as we shared a room. We were encouraged to read and books were readily available as well as paper and pencils, crayons and musical instruments. In many ways, it was an enriched environment.

I had chores to do, as any farm kid does. But I learned responsibility and learned to care for people and animals. I loved to debate with my father and I grew up to emulate him in many ways. And my mother, too, much to my chagrin!

What's so bad about that?

What I've just done is called **reframing**. Reframing means changing the meaning or interpretation of a situation in order to change one's mind to a more positive perspective about the situation. An example might be someone who fell and broke their ankle. At first the individual may think this is a dreadful thing to happen. But by reframing she may think, well, this gives me the time to read and study, or to develop a capacity for poetry or art which I never had time to do. Or she may meet someone special at a rehabilitation hospital and thus make a new friend for a lifetime. She may think, well, that fall was a good thing after all.

That's an example of reframing. It's a way of interpreting a situation in a different light or "frame" so that one is able to deal with it constructively. The concept "has origins in family systems therapy and the work of Virginia Satir. Milton H. Erickson has been associated with reframing... provocative therapy uses reframing with an emphasis on humor." (source: http://en.wikipedia.org/wiki/Reframing)

In that manner, as well, future situations may be thought of as more positive. It's a way of seeing the glass half full rather than half empty, or on the other hand, as in Kenna's situation, she sees her glass as being filled to running over, and that is also a true interpretation as her history reveals. It could have been so much worse. Her future could have ended in death or disaster, that's how sick she was and how dysfunctional.

However, the early childhoods of people later diagnosed with schizophrenia have been demonstrated to affect the occurrence of the illness in later life. "Recent studies have indicated that children who grow up in enriched educational, nutritional and social environments have lower rates of mental illnesses and anti-social behavior that are common precursors to schizophrenia." (source: http://www.schizophrenia.com/prevention)

The role of family and friends in later years is also crucial, we believe. Social support and acceptance for who we are as people, lack of isolation, a nurturing environment with shared dreams and hopes - this is important to any human being on our beautiful Mother, the blue-green Earth. We must learn to give back to society, starting with our family and friends. We must learn it is not all about us. And yet, in a way, isn't it all about us? Are we at times not islands after all?

Social support networks like the Schizophrenia Society of Alberta and its Edmonton chapter are very helpful. We meet like-minded people there and receive advice and support that families perhaps don't or can't provide.

"Schizophrenia and other serious brain disorders are an extreme challenge not only for the person afflicted, but for the entire family. It helps a great deal to be able to talk with other people who have, or are, going through the same things that you are - to share tips and local resources in coping, and to work together in getting the best possible treatment in your city or area." (source: http://www.schizophrenia.com/coping.html)

"Both medical research and anecdotal evidence have revealed that a social support network is a vital part of recovery for mental health consumers."

On Kenna's personal blog a young woman from a country she won't identify posted looking for other people with her particular disability of schizophrenia. She had a link to her blog and although she posts infrequently, Kenna found it exciting that another fellow traveler on this lonely road had found her and was reaching out.

She's a University student in her foreign country and engaged to be married. How wonderful for her. We hope she's happy and we hope she takes her medications and doesn't have a relapse. We hope she has a glorious future with her fiancé, who appears to be a great support for her.

We are so happy when we meet someone at the SSA who shares our struggles, thoughts and feelings. We're intelligent and questioning people and we need our friends and family, and a social network that reaches out beyond boundaries. We need understanding and compassion. It gets lonely here in our little crazy world.

What about formal education? There are working people, there are students, there are the unemployed. It's difficult with someone with this illness to hold down a job. It's difficult to be a student. It's devastating at times to be unemployed and financially stressed. Would we recommend further formal education at the post-secondary level, with the financial strain it implies, with the mental strain, with the social strain of fitting into an academic environment - YES! It's a great experience and it will broaden your mind. But with a word of caution if that's not your cup of java.

We both have formal educations at the post-secondary level. Austin has a PhD and degrees with Honors. Kenna has a BA with Distinction. This is important. We met very interesting and helpful individuals through our education and we learned a lot. We're better off for our education. Kenna always says it didn't get her a job but it helped her think. As an author that's crucial. Kenna earned her degree for the love of learning, not expecting a reward.

But there's a cliché called "the school of hard knocks." It's a cliché because it's so true…we admire those who can sell life insurance to better someone's life or their survivors' lives. We admire a truck driver or a bus driver who can steer that behemoth through a labyrinth of streets and narrow bridges and park it safely. We admire the mail carriers who confront large dogs and blistering heat in summer, and icy sidewalks and deep snow in winter.

Kenna admires her father and those of his generation who had no more than a Grade 8 education yet raised a family and built a home and an inheritance through hard work and native cleverness.

Think what kind of education you want. Is it bringing you closer or further from your dreams?

"Too much of what is called 'education' is little more than an expensive isolation from reality."—Thomas Sowell

Come out of the shadows. Come out of the ivory tower. Get an education sure; it helps you think; it helps you get a good job. It makes you more interesting. It gives you something to do. But does "education" have to mean formal education?

Your hobbies are educating you. Your children are educating you. Your wife or husband and your parents are educating you. The books you read and the shows you watch are educating you. The friends you choose should "make your heart sing." Educate yourself on nutrition, fitness and health. They will feed your body and soul forever. Nourish your spirituality.

We have considered the role of early environment; the roles of family and friends, the roles of learning and social networks and spirituality. Now we ponder the role of **culture**. Of cultural differences and cultural uniqueness.

"Isolation is a dream killer" —Al Joaquin

Statistics show there is an increased incidence of schizophrenia amongst recent immigrants and landed immigrant populations.

"Increased incidence of schizophrenia is observed among some immigrant groups in Europe, with the offspring of immigrants, i.e. "second-generation" immigrants particularly vulnerable. Few contemporary studies have evaluated the risk of schizophrenia among second-generation immigrants in other parts of the world." (source: Cheryl Corcoran et al, *Schizophrenia Bulletin*, http://schizophreniabulletin.oxfordjournals.org/)

Furthermore, closer to the hearth on which we Canadians warm our feet, "The risk for schizophrenia in immigrants to Europe is approximately three times that of native-born populations. Discrimination and marginalization may influence the risk for schizophrenia within migrant populations. The primary objective of the present study was to determine whether the risk associated with migration was also evident 100 years ago. A second objective was to determine whether changing social stresses are associated with changes to the incidence of schizophrenia." (source: G.N. Smith et al, "The incidence of schizophrenia in European immigrants to Canada", *Schizophrenia Research*, Volume 87, Issue 1 , Pages 205-211, October 2006.)

The researchers concluded that "Migration was a risk factor for schizophrenia a century ago as it is today. This risk occurred in white migrants from Europe and increased during a period of increased social stress."

Therefore, there appears to be a greater than average risk for schizophrenia within an immigrant population even in the second generation, and in both Europe (Israel) and Canada, probably due to social isolation or social stress.

Austin's experience is that schizophrenia increases in first generation, not for the parents, but for the first generation with parents that are immigrants. Partially, he says, it's because you're torn between two cultures. He has a good friend who has Generalized Anxiety Disorder, some of which may be due to the fact that he was born in China and emigrated as a baby. He is now in his forties.

Austin's first wife was a Chinese immigrant who suffered greatly from cultural maladaptation. People would lump her normal behavior, which was culturally different, into the madness. Therefore, what people see as erratic behavior they categorized as mental illness.

For example, Austin says he is first generation. His father was born in Texas but essentially raised in England so he is an immigrant. His mother was American but his father was British. His mother's father was British and he was always looking to the Old Country like Austin's father does, which can get you into a fictitious element or "rose colored" glasses.

The Old Country is not the reality of it, they don't realize if it ever existed, it hasn't existed for 50 years but they don't appreciate that. Like in the Bible, they talk about Ruth, "your country is my country." Like Ruth and Naomi, one mistake with multiculturalism is that people don't realize they can't "go home," nor can their children. If they do manage to go home it's not the same and they aren't treated the same. They've changed, as well.

There's a theory that Austin heard on the BBC when he was in Scotland that there's an increased rate of mental illness in North America because of immigration. People who are likely to be immigrants are more likely to have bipolar spectrum type of illnesses because they're more adventurous. So you have a gene pool of 300 million people who all come from people who will take risks, and are adventurous.

As you go West, you find the more adventurous people are in California, so often you get the most risk takers there.

People say that America has more - for example - bipolar than the rest of the world because of its immigrant stock. It's being selected out. That's an interesting theory. There is something that seems almost mentally ill to leave a perfectly good place and go to a completely different place for no good reason. You must have a reason to leave. You may leave because of wars, for example, then you get mental risk to the generations from the damage from the wars or tribulations and stress.

Austin thinks that Ukrainian immigrant people still suffer the effects of the famine 70 years ago, just as Jewish people suffer the effects culturally and psychologically of the Holocaust. These circumstances affect them psychologically. That's a real thing: people tried to ex-terminate them, so that affected them. It fits into the biopsychosocial model, the theory.

Austin knows someone who was an immigrant who suffered a lot of effects. He couldn't understand why he couldn't do well. Immigrants think it's easier to succeed than it is in reality, as it's more compli-cated. They think if you get a degree, for example, you're going to succeed and become a millionaire. Some get very upset when they don't succeed.

People are amazed that Austin can be happy living in a marginal area of the city when he has a PhD. They think he will believe he is a failure. But when he meets professors and he tells them about his research, hopefully, if they understand his academic contribution, they realize he's an equal. He may not be teaching or doing full time research because of his disability, but he is an equal.

However, people define and value things by money and Austin thinks that schizophrenia's stigma is worse than the actual illness. Stigma and discrimination of mental illness are rampant, especially in immigrant communities. Austin thinks that in spite of how badly the mainstream culture treats the mentally ill, to be honest, many immigrant and minority groups treat the mentally ill much worse.

For example, a mutual friend of Austin's who is an immigrant thinks Austin is a malingerer because Austin is not working. Yet if you took a picture of Austin's brain, it would be probably look different from a normal brain. He's had his brain scanned and the ventricles and so on are physically different. The fact that he can get up in the morning and not just stay in bed all day is a miracle. God has blessed him with the capability to function as well as he does. Perhaps he can't take a shower every day. Maybe he can't drive or work, but at least he is trying to be a vital member of society.

Austin observes that we should not judge people on their success but whether they are trying or not. Whether they're volunteering or trying to make a contribution, not whether they actually live up to a set of standards. The irony is, this fellow who is an immigrant is not working. So he looks at Austin, who is volunteering and advocating, and considers Austin as being a malingerer and a negative influence, whereas he isn't working himself.

Before Austin became sick, when he had two Master's degrees, the only job he could get was working at 7-Eleven. He worked there, he worked as sanitation engineer, and whatever job he could take he did, such as dishwasher and so on, and Austin says it was a pretty negative experience before he got sick.

He believes it was probably a contributing factor in his illness, not because those jobs are any lesser, as he felt a sense of dignity working, but because his friends and people around him would laugh at him and say, "Well, you have all this education and the only job you can get is dishwasher." It's probable that was because people in job interviews could recognize there was something odd about him, Austin believes, and so wouldn't hire him.

Cultural factors in psychiatric disorders have been reported by Wolfgang G. Jilek et al

(source: http://www.mentalhealth.com/mag1/wolfgang.html)

in their paper presented at the 26th Congress of the World Federation for Mental Health, July 2001. "Schizophrenic patients in Western developed countries showed a higher frequency of depressive symptoms, primary delusions, thought insertion and thought broadcasting, while in non-Western developing countries visual and directed auditory hallucinations were more frequent [SARTORIUS et al. 1986; JABLENSKY et al 1992]

In a special comparative study of DOSMED conducted in Agra, India, and Ibadan, Nigeria, important differences in the manifestations of schizophrenia were found, which led the investigators to conclude that the content of psychotic symptoms tends to identify critical problems existing in a particular culture [KATZ et al. 1988]."

"That the influence of ethnicity and culture on psychopathology weighs more than geographic proximity, historical relations and racial similarity, became evident in studies which demonstrated significant differences in the symptoms of schizophrenia when comparing patients in Malta and Libya, Japan and China, Korea and China [MASLOWSKI 1986; FUJIMORI et al. 1987; KIM et al. 1993]. Ethnic and cultural differences are reflected in the schizophrenic symptom profiles even if the populations adhere to the same religion, as revealed in the findings of a comparative study of patients in Pakistan and Saudi Arabia [AHMED & NAEEM 1984].

"Psychiatrists working in the so-called Third World have often reported the clinical impression of a more favorable prognosis of schizophrenia among non-Western populations." (source: http://www.mentalhealth.com/mag1/wolfgang.html). Thus, cultural differences appear to be reflected in these findings. What about cultural uniqueness or similarities? It's said that minority groups are more prone to mental illness than the general population, as well, perhaps because of the stress of trying to fit into a culture that may not understand or accept them readily, and the language and religious difficulties that sometime arise as well. This is part of the biopsychosocial aspect of schizophrenia, not an inherent weakness in the genes of such groups. As has been said before, the incidence of schizophrenia remains fairly steady at approximately 1 percent of every country.

"For as he thinketh in his heart, so is he."—(Proverbs 23-7 KJV)
Symptoms of mental illness are different in other countries, and treatments are different, which North American doctors "are only recently beginning to appreciate". However, we have unique indigenous cultures in Canada as well, the First Nations and Inuit, of whom "it is widely recognized that the cultural uniqueness of American Indians and Alaska Natives must be reflected in the methods of diagnosing and treating their mental health problems, but empirical validation of specific diagnostic instruments and treatment has been slow in coming." (source: http://psychservices.psychiatryonline.org/cgi/content/abstract/38/2/165)

"*Oppressed people can't remain oppressed forever.*" —Martin Luther King Jr.

Member comments online indicate that the Diagnostic Statistical Manual - the DSM-IV "cautions psychotherapists to consider clients' personal and cultural uniqueness before deciding whether or not a diagnosable mental illness is [appropriate]..." (source: *Journal article; Annals of the American Psychotherapy Association, Vol. 4, 2001*).

Of course, we are all unique and a person who has schizophrenia is even more unique. The personal uniqueness should always be taken into account, but there does appear to be evidence for cultural differences and cultural uniqueness.

Chapter 5:
Spirituality

A child came home from Sunday School and told his mother that he had learned a new song about a cross-eyed bear named Gladly. It was a while before she realized that the hymn was "Gladly The Cross I'd Bear."

A close relationship between religious delusions and schizophrenia has been observed. Clients who "hear God's voice" or believe they are Jesus Christ or God or the Archangel Gabriel, or see the Antichrist can become violent: homicidal or suicidal. "God's voice" may tell them to stop taking their medication, or pluck out an eye, for example, or another violent act.

"In a study of inpatients with schizophrenia, conducted by Siddle and Haddock, et al., those with religious delusions were the most severely ill with religious delusions that were more frequently observed and lasted for longer periods of time." (source: http://www.sciforums.com/showthread.php?t=51361)

"*I reject any religious doctrine that does not appeal to reason and is in conflict with morality.*" —Mohandas Gandhi

Austin thinks the reason so many people with schizophrenia and bipolar illness have religious visions and delusions is because religion and spirituality are such powerful healing experiences. We want to know why we die and what happens afterwards, the meaning of life and its explanation. We need to accept it except this belief gets misfired in the mind of people who have delusions. They think it's a message from God and is like a delusion of grandeur as you get self-referential thinking. That's where everything is referred to the self.

For example, while visiting his wife in the hospital in June 2011, Austin began to get breakthrough symptoms and thought the nurses were talking about him when he heard them in the hallway.

Kenna has also experienced that symptom, where somebody laughs and she thinks it's about her. It's annoying, and Austin tells himself, "Well, this is just..." but you still think it. It comes in and you think it. You have to say, "Well, this isn't logical. This person's a stranger and stuff."

But then, on the other hand, Austin is 6 feet 5 inches tall, 400 pounds, and people do stare. He laughs at himself, and observes that people do look at him and so that's real, so sometimes he doesn't pay attention. If he doesn't shower for a while, people pay attention to him, and are actually looking at him or commenting on him. So it could be real. So Austin can't distinguish when it's real and when it isn't. So he just ignores it all.

Sometimes when people whisper things to him or give him quiet messages, he doesn't pay attention. They might think he's an oaf because he doesn't take a hint, but with Austin you must be forthright.

Kenna noticed that as soon as a person is forthright with Austin he will correct himself and do his best. Kenna may be the same way but she hasn't noticed it. Perhaps both of them don't pick up on nuances. That's associated with schizophrenia and schizotypal personalities, according to Austin.

There's probably a whole world of people, a certain large percentage of the population have schizophrenia-like symptoms. For example, Austin says, 4 percent of the population hears voices but only 1 percent of the population has schizophrenia. So there's 3 percent of the population who are hearing voices but aren't schizophrenic. Perhaps more, he says, perhaps 5 percent or 6 percent. So that's interesting. It's not all just about hearing voices. People think, oh, you hear voices, you're schizophrenic. That's not what schizophrenia is. It's more than that. People get confused that way.

What would cause people to hear voices? Maybe it's a message from God or a message connecting to spirituality, Austin muses. We are spiritual beings, he says, and maybe the unconscious is very powerful. Maybe our unconscious is trying to tell us things.

For example, his wife had a nightmare the night before she was taken to hospital. It woke her up, saying that she was going to get her leg amputated. Then six hours later the doctors were getting ready to amputate her leg. She dreamed that if she didn't do something to help she was going to lose her leg. Is that a message from God or from the subconscious? Is it prophetic or is it subconscious?

Austin says that God works through the world and we have to accept it and live a moral life, and as good a life as we can under the circumstances. And the world is not perfect and will never be perfect. But all you can do is try to stay healthy and happy.

For example, when Kenna became ill she got involved in the criminal justice system. And that's how she got help, she said. That's sad that she didn't get help before that. It had to get to a crisis. She couldn't be helped before that. Within the last six to ten years, Kenna tried to get help from a competent therapist, and couldn't connect with a psychiatrist. The nurses couldn't help her. Austin observes that he is a very good advocate and can help.

Austin has religious visions. Kenna had those and thought she was a special agent of God. We all are special agents of God in a way. Austin thinks it's a miracle he woke up this morning. It's a miracle his house is clean. You don't have to look for nuclear explosions to realize the miracle of life; just being in existence is enough.

Could counseling by a priest or minister have been beneficial for Kenna, or would they perhaps have encouraged the delusion? Some ministers Kenna saw were encouraging a delusion, and that was actually a negative thing because it encouraged the illness.

Austin observes you have to be sure of the difference between psychosis and spirituality. He asks Kenna if it was in the Catholic faith, and it was not. However, Christian churches often think people are possessed but we're not possessed, we're in touch with forces that short-circuit our brain.

Most people just turn it off and put up filters. We don't have those filters to prevent that image from getting into us and it just short-circuits us. After all, as a moral being, can we see God? If we saw God in His entirety, we would vaporize, so we have to see God through shadows, signs or imagination.

Can we see God directly? Catholics believe that only some saints see God and most saints are very strange, says Austin.

Kenna notes that if Jesus Christ were alive today and on earth he would probably be locked up in a mental institution. Christians visit people in jails but they seldom visit psychiatric wards. Some priests or ministers will visit, but very few parishioners, as members of the congregation do not normally visit psychiatric wards. They will visit jails but they are frightened to visit those with mental illness.

Austin postulates the reason people are so frightened of mental illness is they realize how close they are to becoming sick themselves. They think this person could be me, and that scares them.

The information found in this chapter concerning the role of the church, individual spirituality and the role of the pastor in counseling and spiritual direction must be taken with circumspection.

Our hesitation to recommend spiritual counseling and support for schizophrenia through formal religion is supported by research such as that of an ongoing study with Mohr S and Huguelet P. "The relationship between schizophrenia and religion and its implications for care." *Swiss Med Wkly* 2004;134:369-376 We may reach the conclusion that "For their patients with schizophrenia, psychiatrists believe that religion and spirituality cannot be used as tools for ongoing social support as they can lead to a more pathological condition." . (source:

http://www.sciforums.com/showthread.php?t=51361) In other words, a worsening of psychotic symptoms.

Thus, we proffer with hesitation the following suggestions on the usefulness of religion as a therapeutic device or tool of enlightenment. Perhaps the therapist might work with the delusion in a curative setting such as Cognitive Behavioral Therapy (CBT) and turn it around by adjusting the client's thought processes directed towards his particular understanding of religion or spirituality.

The role of the church includes group support, friendships in church and supportive mantras or slogans to live by as well as the use of prayer and meditation or contemplation exercises, with the goal of healing or amelioration. Some churches practice laying on of hands or "faith healing," anointing with oil and so on; even exorcism in extreme cases. Some of these interventions have been shown to be actually dangerous and exacerbate the symptoms.

"A Romanian priest and four nuns were recently sentenced in the killing of a nun, Maricica Cornici, who had been treated for schizophrenia. When the ill nun relapsed and believed she heard the devil talking to her, the priest and attending nuns attempted to perform a brutal exorcism on her in an attempt to drive out the devil. This"exorcism" is what ultimately caused the nun's death, it was determined. " (source:

http://www.schizophrenia.com/sznews/archives/004675.html)

"The Vatican issued new guidelines in 1999 urging priests to take modern psychiatry into account before deciding who should be exorcised."

The role of individual spirituality includes one's spiritual and emotional strength as part of the constellation of factors: physical, mental, emotional and spiritual elements necessary for optimum health. Members tend to be strengthened by participation in their respective religious practices and faith (at least that is the goal).

Early family environment plays a significant part in deciding in which faith (or not) the individual is instructed and nurtured. There are numerous different religions throughout our nation, the member's nation of origin, and the world.

The world's major religions include Christianity, Islam, Buddhism, Hinduism (the world's oldest religion and with approximately a billion adherents, found mainly in India and Nepal), Judaism, Baha'i, Confucianism, Janaism (one of the world's oldest religions and found in India), and Shinto. (source: http://listverse.com/2007/07/31/top-10-organized-religions-and-their-core-beliefs/)

"All major religious traditions carry basically the same message, that is love, compassion and forgiveness; the important thing is they should be part of our daily lives." —Dalai Lama

Priests, gurus, pastors, ministers, lay ministers and other spiritual leaders play a major role in spiritual guidance and direction. As well, many will provide counseling with the emphasis, of course, on their particular faith. It is hoped the counseling would be tempered with wisdom and that the appropriate training and therapeutic skills be employed.

Faith and reason combined, tolerance for differences, "love, compassion and forgiveness..." These attributes can't help but be helpful, in our view.

As with other spiritual modalities listed above, each faith is unique to the individual who practices it and as such will moderate the appearance of his religious delusions. However, a word of caution from studies such as that quoted at the beginning of this chapter. "Religious delusions are clinically important because they may be associated with self-harm and poorer outcomes from treatment. They have not been extensively researched...Religious delusions are commonly found in schizophrenia and by comparison with other patients who have schizophrenia, those patients with religious delusions appear to be more severely ill. This warrants further investigation." (source: "Religious delusions in patients admitted to hospital with schizophrenia." Siddle R, Haddock G, Tarrier N, Faragher EB. Department of Clinical Psychology, North Manchester General Hospital, Crumpsall, UK.)

Some would argue the existence of a malevolent force or a God who speaks to his people, and back it up with their particular scriptures.

God enters by a private door into every individual. —Ralph Waldo Emerson

Chapter 6:
Stigma and Harassment

"One kind word can warm three winter months."—Japanese proverb

Sticks and Stones can break my bones
But names will never h-u-r-ttt me...
Oh, yeah?

Austin relates, "In the 1890s, after giving birth to her second child, my great-grandmother developed what today is called schizophrenia. For all intents and purposes, her life was over. Stricken with this mental illness, known at the time as dementia praecox, she was put away in an asylum and left to die some decades later in southern England. During this time, her husband rose in the ranks as a London police officer, divorced his ill wife, and remarried.

Schizophrenia reappeared in my family two generations later. After the birth of her third child, my mother developed postpartum depression that eventually cascaded into the psychosis of schizophrenia. And although I was only five at the time, I remember this tumultuous time for our family.

"My mother, who never responded well to medication, was in and out of hospitals for the majority of my childhood. To this day, our family continues to bear the brunt of hostility from the small Alberta town I grew up in due to our family's perceived strange behavior.

"The torments I was subjected to in school were nightmarish and brutal. And for whatever reasons, the teachers did nothing to protect me from the endless physical, verbal and emotional lashings that my peers endlessly bestowed upon me.

"But those school days would prepare me well for the ostracism I would later receive when I myself became afflicted with schizophrenia at 30. One year after graduating with a bachelor's (degree) in geography, I found myself living in a tent near the South Pole on an expedition recovering meteorites for NASA. Although I was constantly confronted with dangerously freezing temperatures and situations in which my life was severely threatened, I did not fear dying. Rather, I experienced nightmares. The shame of my school days had begun manifesting itself: like my mother before me, I was becoming insane.

"After my first psychotic episode, several family members insisted I get sterilized, claiming I was genetically inferior. Geneticists have also expressed this opinion to me.

"I have often likened this to the Nazis who used castration or murder in an attempt to eliminate further schizophrenia or other mental disabilities. Even Alberta had its own eugenic laws in my father's time.

"People have called me courageous for advocating for schizophrenics and the seriously mentally ill. It is not courage, rather a deep-seated fear of the consequences of the social and personal isolation experienced by schizophrenics that fuels my passion.

I tell my wife that I missed out on a 20-year period of work that my contemporaries are now concluding by gazing at their fast approaching retirements. In contrast, my wife and I will likely face a retirement below the poverty line. I hear people grumble about their poverty while earning $50,000 annually. Yet for the vast majority of people receiving Assured Income for the Severely Handicapped (AISH), such richness is an unattainable dream.

"After my investiture as a Member of the Order of Canada in 2007, relatives were incensed that the Mardon name was linking the esteemed Canadian honour with the shame of schizophrenia. An estimated one per cent of the population suffers from schizophrenia. Up to 90 per cent of those afflicted do not take their medications properly. I am in the slim minority who take their medications properly. But I want that number to change. I have experienced and witnessed firsthand what happens to the afflicted who do not take their medication — be it due to shame, neglect, fear, or lack of support.

"It is ironic that for the entire history of our species there was no treatment for schizophrenia except faith and time and today when there are treatments that manage this chronic lifelong illness, the vast majority of those who are ill today do not properly avail themselves of these treatments but instead keep visiting the well of madness by not taking their medication properly.

"If I had taken the other path of not taking the antipsychotic medications, instead of having dinner with doctors tonight, I would very likely be having dinner with my fellow schizophrenics at a soup kitchen and sleeping on a grate or a box in a back alley. I have chosen sanity over that. That is one of the reasons I speak out about schizophrenia.

"Even on medication, I experience paranoia, have visions and hear voices. And while society may never classify me as "normal," I strive to maintain, with my wife's support, my health and live a useful, happy life."

Austin states he has been receiving AISH since 1993. He has been in social housing and lived in substandard housing and basement suites, owned a house with his first wife and had some problems with ownership of a house that his family owned, that he lost custody of.

Now that his present wife and he own their own condominium, their friends say now that you own the place, you should move up. Get a bigger place. Get a better place. They accept their modest belongings because they are both on assistance. Austin observes they should live in this neighborhood because they're on AISH and they wouldn't have anything in common with more well to do neighbors. They can access the LRT and that's a reason why the homeless congregate in that area. There is so much social housing because it's convenient without a car. A grocery store is just a quarter of a block away, a restaurant and a bank are nearby, and so on, and they have been able to build up equity in their home.

Beyond that, they have the security of knowing their rent is not going to go up. Renters don't have that security, and with the labor crunch, it will likely happen within the next couple of years that rents will increase again. People were removed from their longstanding homes when apartments were made into condominiums.

People they know have lost houses. Austin and his wife have been made homeless over the years. They have had disasters. Most people don't appreciate the difficulties they've faced. Still, they try to be proactive.

Austin approached 10 mortgage companies to get financing when they moved into their present home, and they all said no. They were able to get a private mortgage through a realtor and that saved their bacon. Then a year and a half later, once they owned the property, they were able to get a mortgage.

His wife found this place which they presently own. It's accessible. She uses a wheelchair occasionally and there are no stairs; it's very comfortable, and outwardly attractive. There's security and it looks nice. The insulation is poor, Austin says, but the sound is quite well insulated. The insulation for the heat is poor and people on the second and third floor notice it as being too hot or too cold during the summer or winter. They live on the first floor so don't notice it.

What else? Being on a fixed income on AISH, they've had to use the Food Bank and charity; collect pop bottles in the alley. Austin says they've paid their mortgage with pop bottles. They just did whatever it took to survive. His wife makes his underwear and recycles old tee-shirts. They try to save as much as they can. For example, when he goes out for a meal, Austin tries to order at least one step down, so if everyone else orders a meal, Austin orders soup. If they order soup, he has toast and coffee, or a coffee.

If he goes out, he still has coffee as that is his one luxury. He feels guilty for spending money on coffee but, he points out, he has to socialize. It's not a cappuccino.

This winter he ordered three hot chocolates because his wife wasn't home at the time so he went over to Starbucks and on three separate occasions ordered a hot chocolate. He felt very bad about that but it was more comforting than regular coffee. For example, he orders a grande coffee in an avente cup then puts lots of milk in it so it tastes better than a regular coffee. He likes lots of skim milk.

There are strategies for saving money that Kenna uses herself. But Austin thinks they have been able to cope. Between his wife and himself - she has an acquired brain injury and he has schizophrenia - they can solve a problem. For example, his wife doesn't talk on the phone because of her PTST. He talks on the phone and speaks to people when he needs to. He thinks he probably calls his worker too much. Austin chuckles.

On AISH you get a half discount on the buses and they use that. His wife uses DATS and gets the DATS free but has to pay each time she uses it as a user fee. Also, people on AISH get a free leisure pass with the City of Edmonton.

Chapter 7:
The Perception of Violence

"Perfumes are the feelings of flowers."—Heinrich Heine

"Believing he was acting on orders from God, Vincent Li attacked a stranger on a Greyhound bus last summer, mutilating his victim before decapitating him and cannibalizing part of the body.

"In a clear voice, Li pleaded not guilty Tuesday in Winnipeg to a charge of second-degree murder in the death of 22-year-old Timothy McLean of Winnipeg on a Greyhound bus in Manitoba last July.

"The Crown and Defence have agreed on a statement of facts read to the court on Tuesday that suggests Li was mentally ill at the time of the slaying... and forensic psychiatrist Dr. Stanley Yaren gave evidence that Li was diagnosed as schizophrenic and suffering a major psychotic episode — tormented by auditory hallucinations — at the time of the killing." (source: CBC News March 3, 2008)."

A personal vignette from Kenna's experience seems to support the idea of the general public's perception of increased risk of violence in people with schizophrenia and lack of compassion for them. An acquaintance expressed concern to her that a person with a mental illness would ever be released from hospital or jail again after a violent episode, as she couldn't be sure they would comply with treatment and not reoffend. This is a personal and individual response but somewhat typical of individuals Kenna has spoken with over the years.

It would seem there is less sympathy for the mentally ill offender and less willingness to extend rehabilitation services to them, or to acknowledge that they are as worthy of mercy and justice than for the violent offender from the general population who does not have schizophrenia.

It would seem, perhaps from the nature of their crimes, and the blatant media coverage slashed across headlines of "former mental patient" or "schizophrenic says God told him to kill" - that the general public is under the impression that all schizophrenics are violent, or that those who do commit violent acts can't be rehabilitated and can't feel remorse. They can and do.

"He's not an animal," a young male acquaintance said to Kenna about Vincent Li. "My co-workers think he shouldn't be allowed to walk on the grounds and should be kept in his cell like an animal. He's sick. He's a human being." This young man has an unusually compassionate approach to the problem of possible relapse of a mentally ill offender, and to the treatment of Vincent Li while he is held indefinitely in a Forensic Hospital (formerly known sometimes as a Hospital for the Criminally Insane).

Of note, Vincent Li asked the police officers who arrested him to kill him. He committed a heinous act of violence. Will he offend again? Will the "lifers" in the general population in maximum security prisons offend again? Statistics show there is little probability.

Studies do show that "It is now accepted that people with schizophrenia are significantly more likely to be violent than other members of the general population..."

However, "The proportion of violent crime in society attributable to schizophrenia consistently falls below 10% ...

"Of the 17% of patients with a diagnosis of schizophrenia, 9% were violent in the first 20 weeks after discharge. This compares with a violence prevalence of 19% for depression, 15% for bipolar disorder,

17.2% for other psychotic disorders, 29% for substance misuse disorders and 25% for personality disorder alone..." (source: *The British Journal of Psychiatry* (2002) 180: 490-495, "Violence and schizophrenia: examining the evidence" Walsh, Elizabeth; Buchanan, Alec; Fahy, Thomas.) "The risk of violence is multiplied by concurrent substance abuse disorders" (source: Arseneault et al., 2000; Steadman et al., 1998).

Schizophrenia and the Police: Personal anecdotal experience of people with schizophrenia would seem to indicate that schizophrenics are treated as being less credible than the general population and with less sympathy. Studies don't support that view.

A recent study concluded that "a person with schizophrenia was viewed by the police officers in this study as being less responsible, more deserving of pity, and more worthy of help than a person without a mental illness label." (source: Psychiatr Serv 55:49-53, January 2004. "Police Officers' Attitudes Toward and Decisions About Persons With Mental Illness", Amy C. Watson, Ph.D., Patrick W. Corrigan, Psy.D. and Victor Ottati, Ph.D.).

In our experience the police force in our city is compassionate and professional in their dealings with the mentally ill. Often the homeless are simply relocated or given a cell for the night to keep safe.

Mental Health Act and Falling Between the Cracks:
FACS (Forensic Assessment Community Services) offers psychiatric assessment and counseling for people with mental illness who have been referred through the courts. The Schizophrenia Society of Alberta is well aware of the efficiency and excellence of the services at FACS. Why put a mentally ill person in jail? She needs treatment and yes, in the case of a violent crime, incarceration in a Forensic Hospital for an indefinite period of time until deemed safe to return to the community. Still, where are the people with schizophrenia in America today?

- 6% are homeless or live in shelters

- 6% live in jails or prisons

- 5% to 6% live in Hospitals

- 10% live in Nursing homes

- 25% live with a family member

- 8% are living independently

- 0% live in Supervised Housing (group homes, etc.)

(Source: "Surviving Schizophrenia"
http://www.schizophrenia.com/media/#intro)

"However, detainees with mental disorders or substance abuse disorders are often in jail because of non-violent crimes" (source: http://www.iafmhs.org/files/Stadtlandspr05.pdf)
(Teplin, 1994).

In studies, psychopathic traits (antisocial/unstable lifestyle) are strongly associated with violent recidivism (reoffenses) rather than interpersonal or affective traits. (source: *International Journal of Forensic Mental Health* 2005, Vol. 4, No. 1, pages 89-97 ©2005 International Association of Forensic Mental Health Services, Psychopathic Traits and Risk of Criminal Recidivism in Offenders with and without Mental Disorders, Cornelis Stadtland, Nikolaus Kleindienst, Carolin Kröner, Matthias Eidt, and Norbert Nedopil)

In group 1 consisting of participants who met criteria for major mental disorders,

- 45 (17.2%) did not reoffend,

- 13 (5.0%) reoffended non-violently,

- 9 (3.4%) reoffended violently and

- 5 offenders with schizophrenia re-offended.

In group2,

- 57 (21.8%) of the defendants with personality disorders, substance abuse or a co-morbidity did not reoffend,

- 8 (14.5%) had a non-violent re-offence and

- 16 (6.1%) a violent re-offense.

In group 3, which included offenders without any psychiatric disorder,

- 57 (21.8%) did not reoffend,

- 15 (5.7%) reoffended with non-violent crimes and

- (2.7%) exhibited violent re-offenses.

Compared to offenders without psychiatric co-morbidity, relative risks for a re-offense were 1.21 and 1.74 for offenders with major mental disorders and for offenders with personality disorders or substance abuse, respectively.

Kenna has been subjected to discrimination and hostility in regard to her scrapes with the law as a result of her delusional illness. She is helpless to defend herself at these times other than to try to explain to those who aren't capable of understanding a delusional illness that she isn't a bad nor a violent person, and that this is a result of illness. Understanding? It is rare.

Chapter 8:
Financial Concerns

"It isn't the mountain ahead that wears you out; it's the grain of sand in your shoe."
-Robert W. Service

Few people with schizophrenia are able to work full-time. Some hold down part-time jobs; many who do are under-employed. Factors against full-time, financially and emotionally rewarding employment for those with schizophrenia include negative symptoms of apathy, withdrawal and limited emotional expression; possibility of relapse while on the job and thus inappropriate behavior; side effects of medications including sedation and lack of concentration; decline in cognitive skills or lack of concentration required for a profession or trade; odd behavior; poor social skills; not owning a vehicle; not having a valid driver's license; living too far from suitable work such as a rural area; a criminal record making it difficult to find employment; or social stigma and discrimination associated with a diagnosis of mental illness. "Companies are less likely to hire people with schizophrenia because employers see them as incapable of holding down a job." (source: http://www.schizophrenia.com/sznews/archives/001946.html)

Probably the most well-known celebrity is John Nash, whose struggles with paranoid schizophrenia were portrayed by Russell Crowe in the movie "A Beautiful Mind". Although highly fictionalized, the movie brought some notoriety to the Nobel Laureate winner and mathematician, who at 72 years of age is still working as an academic and researcher. Well known or famous people with schizophrenia or suspected of having schizophrenia are listed as follows. (source: http://www.schizophrenia.com/famous.htm\#tom)

- Tom Harrell, Jazz Musician

- Meera Popkin, Broadway Star

- John Nash - Mathematician/Nobel Prize Winner

- Albert Einstein's son - Eduard Einstein

- Dr. James Watson's son (Dr. Watson is co-discover of DNA and Nobel Prize winner)

- Alan Alda's Mother (Alan Alda is the famous TV actor from the series MASH)

- Andy Goram - Scottish Soccer Player/Goal Keeper

- Lionel Aldridge - Superbowl-winning Football Player

- Peter Green, Guitarist for the band Fleetwood Mac

- Syd Barrett of the band Pink Floyd

- Alexander "Skip" Spence and Bob Mosley - both members of the 1960's rock group Moby Grape (and Jefferson Airplane for Skip Spence)

- Roger Kynard "Rocky" Erickson, of the Austin-based 1960's group The Thirteenth Floor Elevators

- Joe Meek - 1960's British record producer

- James Beck Gordon (Jim Gordon) - James Gordon had been, quite simply, one of the greatest drummers of his time

- Charles "Buddy" Bolden - Jazz Musician

- Antoin Artaud - Dramatist, Artist

- Mary Todd Lincoln, wife of Abraham Lincoln (past-President of the United States)

- Vaclav Nijinsky, Famous Russian Dancer

- Jack Kerouac, Author, was diagnosed with Schizophrenia

- Tennessee Williams' sister Rose Williams had schizophrenia

(source: Tennessee Williams *Notebooks*, Edited by Margaret Bradham Thornton, Yale University Press, 2007)

It seems to us the creative arts are highly represented here including musicians, artists, authors, as well as mathematicians and athletic figures.

The majority of people with schizophrenia, however, are in low-paying or part-time jobs, and many do not or cannot work outside the home at all. As schizophrenia typically hits at a young age, between 18 and 25 years old in males, and by 30 years old in females (an average age), the possibilities for higher education are limited due to the time span in which the individual is typically acutely ill. The percentage of people with schizophrenia living in poverty is quite high. There are disability pensions available such as AISH (Assured Income for the Severely Handicapped) in Alberta and CPP (Canada Pension Plan) disability benefits in Canada. The eligibility for these pensions must be reviewed regularly by a physician and Kenna finds this to be humiliating although she can see where a regular review is necessary.

When Kenna had her second mental breakdown in 1990 she was working for the University of Alberta and was put on a disability pension for two years. She worked during this time at part-time jobs, and a percentage of her wages were deducted from the pension. As well, the workplace stipulated that Kenna apply for Canada Pension Plan disability to supplement the income supplied by the university's insurance company. This involved the knowledge of Kenna's employers as the CPP contacted her employers for confirmation as well. It would obviously have been more beneficial for her not to have worked at all.

Fortunately, she was able to stand on her own feet after two years, working at three part time jobs until finally she started full time at one of them a couple of years later. She worked there for eight years then began her own home based medical transcription business, working part-time at first to supplement the meager income this brought in until her company became profitable.

Evidence-based research indicates that it's beneficial for those with mental illness to work at an occupation. Being in the workplace engages the mind and creates also a feeling of self-satisfaction, leading to self-esteem. It's difficult to find employers who will hire a person with mental illness; thus, many will hide their illness until they have proven themselves, or until symptoms make themselves evident.

Benefits such as health care and prescription coverage are important to consider, and these are typically covered by disability pensions but not necessarily on the job. Antipsychotic medications and antidepressants are expensive, prohibitively so, and this is a consideration.

"It is estimated that only 10 percent to 27 percent of people with schizophrenia are in the workforce. But in a 2008 survey of those who live with schizophrenia, 76 percent of respondents said they thought having a job would improve their lives." (source: Working With Schizophrenia, by Connie Brichford, Medically Reviewed by Kevin O. Hwang, MD, MPH).

Chapter 9:
Seniors with Schizophrenia

"Grow old along with me. The best is yet to be." - Robert Browning

Statistics are not available for the true percentage of older adults with schizophrenia or other mental illness. It is known that individuals over 60 are more likely to consult their family physicians or healthcare providers than mental health practitioners. Many of the available reports come from family members who might have noticed the change in their parents or grandparents or symptoms and report them, but some must go unreported. (source: Reichel's care of the elderly: clinical aspects of aging By Joseph J. Gallo, William Reichel)

Those seniors with symptoms of chronic schizophrenia have probably been ill for most of their lifetimes, as evidenced by the relatively young age of onset of the illness (between 18 and 25 for males or up to 30 for females on average). By the time they reach 60 or 65 an individual may have suffered cognitive decline or other negative symptoms of the disease, or mood disorders such as depression or anxiety as well as physical health problems brought on by the long-term use of neuroleptic medication.

Side effects of these medications can be serious and shorten a life span or eventually result in kidney or liver failure, diabetes, thyroid problems and other chronic side effects when these heavy medications are taken on a long-term basis. The newer medications have fewer side effects but seniors were started on medications when the medications were relatively new and had more serious side effects.

When Kenna was first diagnosed, she was given Chlorpromazine and later Trilafon, which were called major tranquilizers rather than anti-psychotics. It was like being hit over the head with a hammer. Kenna couldn't navigate stairs nor could she walk properly for more than 10 minutes without having to sleep. Her mouth was so dry that if she drove across town she would have to stop two or three times to buy something to drink. She gained weight around her abdomen in particular.

An antidepressant called Tofranil was added, and another medication to suppress the uncontrollable tremor in her hands. Her face was masklike. She promised herself that she would do anything rather than return to the psychosis which made these medications necessary, and she took the medications until 1990, during which time she had continued to work.

In 1990 Kenna considered herself coping well enough to stop the meds. Well, you know what happened… another breakdown similar to the breakdown in 1975, not as severe, not as violently damaging, but catastrophic just the same. She lost her job, alienated her family and friends, involved the law in a nonviolent way, and slowly made her way back to health with the assistance of a medication called Fluanxol which was administered in a Depot injection, first once a week, then every two weeks.

There's a side effect of long term use of psychotropic medication called tardive dyskinesia, which is involuntary movements of the tongue, lips, puckering of the cheeks, and sometimes movements of the extremities and torso as well. It isn't painful but can be disfiguring and embarrassing, and affects primarily female patients and the elderly who have been taking neuroleptics for a long time. (source: Tardive Dyskinesia, Author: James Robert Brasic, MD, MPH, Assistant Professor, Division of Nuclear Medicine, Russell H Morgan Department of Radiology and Radiological Science, Johns Hopkins University School of Medicine; Coauthor(s): Brian Bronson, MD, Staff Physician, Department of Psychiatry, New York University Medical Center; Tristen T Chun, Division of Nuclear Medicine, Russell H Morgan Department of Radiology and Radiological Science, Johns Hopkins University School of Medicine, http://emedicine.medscape.com/article/1151826-overview) .

Neither Austin nor Kenna have developed obvious signs of this disorder but Kenna does notice movements of her tongue in the interior of her mouth pressing on her left molar teeth which could be a result of taking neuroleptic medications since 1978. A number of medications have been used to try to treat TD but treatment is not always successful.

Again, Kenna uses a cost/benefits analysis as to the emotional or physical cost of taking the medications as prescribed and the benefits of the medications. The medications win. No contest.

Austin promised his wife when they were married that he would faithfully take his medications to control his illness for as long as he lived.

Noncompliance with taking medications as prescribed is a puzzle and an ongoing problem for health care professionals and of course, the families and patients themselves. Noncompliance has been associated with the kind of relationship a patient has with their treating physician or psychiatrist. Frank and Gunderson found that in a therapeutic alliance over 6 months with a therapist "74% of patients with fair or poor therapeutic alliances... failed to comply fully... only 26% of patients with schizophrenia with a good alliance with their therapist were noncompliant."

It's been estimated that up to three times as many people with schizophrenia smoke as in the general population, and researchers theorize it may be a form of self-medication. Does nicotine actually help the symptoms of schizophrenia? (source:

http://www.sfn.org/index.aspx?pagename=brainbriefings_smoking.com) In view of the potentially life threatening side effects of nicotine it would be inadvisable to go down this road even if it were proven to have some beneficial effects.

Austin remembers in former times therapists actually encouraging mentally ill patients to smoke, and cigarettes were freely given out on the psychiatric wards. Thus, it could be postulated that the elderly with schizophrenia probably smoke more than the average population, again lending themselves to risk of physical illness or death.

Isolation is another problem experienced by the elderly in our society and more so by those with mental illness. This leads in a closed loop or Moebius strip to increased risk of cognitive and social decline. It's been estimated that a large percentage of the homeless over age 50 suffer from schizophrenia. Social relationships, so vital to anyone's mental health, may become tenuous in old age due to decreased mobility, illness and fear of falling outside the home, thus causing thus less venturing out and fewer opportunities to mingle.

Friends may pass on and family members may neglect the elderly. If behaviors become increasingly odd, the illness may be confused with dementia or other illnesses and wrongly diagnosed, and thus wrongly treated.

"Research has been largely neglected on the elderly and schizophrenia, the incidence, treatment, causes and management. Over 90% of published papers on schizophrenia have excluded elderly persons with the disorder. Despite this, approximately 23.5% of patients with schizophrenia developed the illness after the age of 40. These persons are considered to have late-onset schizophrenia. Roughly 4% of persons with schizophrenia have onset after the age of 60 and are considered to have very-late-onset schizophrenia.

"Persons who develop schizophrenia before age 45, and who age with it, represent about 85% of all persons with schizophrenia. Overall community prevalence estimates for schizophrenia (both early and late onset) in individuals over the age of 65, however, ranges from only 0.1% to 0.5%. Therefore, while schizophrenia represents a significant cause of psychosis in the elderly, it is not as common a cause of psychosis in the elderly as dementia, depression, and delirium." (source: MedScape Today: The Many Faces of Psychosis in the Elderly: Schizophrenia http://www.medscape.com/viewarticle/564899_6).

Medical supervision and regular lab tests to monitor the effects of their medications is necessary for maintenance of the elderly. It must not be forgotten, however, that in Kenna's opinion there's no reason to anticipate a decline in old age, continued poverty or social isolation.

Years ago, therapists told Kenna she would never work again and that she would be in and out of psychiatric institutions for the rest of her life. She works and will probably continue to work, as John Nash said, until she is 100. She was last hospitalized in 1990, when she quit taking the medication that had been prescribed. She won't make that mistake again.

Today, at age 68 years, Kenna remains interested and healthy. She is happy and comfortable, with many friends and a successful small business. Only within the past two years has she begun to write for publication, finding great joy in this activity which has engaged her interest all her life. She has many published articles, poems, short stories, and two books presently released by her publishers, *Imajin Books* and *Diamond Heart Press*. A diagnosis of schizophrenia is not a death sentence nor does it relegate a person to the fringes of society unless we choose it. It takes lots of hard work, yes, but the elderly can reap the benefits of experience and perhaps a lessening of symptoms, a mellowing as time goes on, and an acceptance.

Companionship and laughter and a knowledge of contributing to society such as volunteering, or learning a new language or a new skill, or a musical instrument, all within the bounds of one's financial ability and competence or interests can be carried on into a very old age until the ends of life itself. More on this later in Chapter 12.

There's no reason a diagnosis of schizophrenia or other mental illness should limit one to the fringes of society, to uselessness, hopelessness, or to sadness and despair. There are many who suffer more physically than we do mentally and emotionally. Our choice of attitude is up to us.

We don't have a terminal illness. All possibilities are open to us and are within the realm of probability with an attitude of gratitude, a joie de vivre, a fighting spirit and a love of oneself. "Loving oneself can develop into a lifetime romance." (Anne Collins)

Remain healthy, remain fit, walk, write poetry, read, play sports, dialogue with your doctor and loved ones. Write your memoirs. Paint. If you have a life companion be grateful. Don't worry, be happy. The best is yet to come.

Villa Caritas, a short-term geriatric facility in Edmonton, Alberta
First published in Edmonton Senior by Kenna McKinnon

Villa Caritas, Covenant Health's new 150-bed facility, is serving a growing number of seniors with complex mental health and medical conditions. There are 9 physicians and 300 staff at Villa Caritas with five 30-bed units. It's a three story 135,000 sq. ft. building with 150 spacious private rooms, each with a large window, storage and a private bathroom.

"I can sleep easy. I don't have to worry about how my wife is taken care of. She sleeps; she's well taken care of; so I can sleep also." Joss Heroux sits across from me in the sunny lobby of Villa Caritas at 88th Avenue and 165th Street. Joss' wife was transferred from Dickinsfield when her Alzheimer's illness became more aggressive. She will be assessed here at Villa Caritas and her medications will be adjusted before she is sent back to the community, perhaps to Dickinsfield or another nursing care center.

Light streams through the large windows of the lobby in which we are seated. Comfortable overstuffed armchairs are scattered about. Staff bustles about the well-appointed Information desk directly across from the front door and the spacious lobby. Gail Tricker, the extremely well qualified and efficient Patient Care Manager, sits beside Joss.

Joss' wife first showed symptoms of Alzheimer's disease, he says, approximately 15 years ago, at a younger age than most. She is presently 63 years old. Joss observes, "From here, once she gets under control with the proper medication, she will be put into a nursing home again."

"It's nice facilities and it's built to accommodate people who have this kind of problem."

Gail affirms that. "Villa Caritas is a 150-bed acute care geriatric psychiatric facility. So that means that there are not any long-term care beds here. Once we manage the patient's illness, the patients will be discharged to the most appropriate setting in the community."

"About 50 percent of our patients…do go back home to independent living."

Joss says of the facility, "People that work here are very caring. Very caring." He indicates that the same staff who worked at Alberta Hospital Edmonton are now working at Villa Caritas, bringing many years of experience, knowledge and education to this new setting.

Two courtyards will be constructed as soon as the ground thaws this spring, enabling outdoor access for the patients. The location also enables access to the nearby West Edmonton Mall, the community, and transit services if appropriate.

Are there weekend and holiday passes for the patients at Villa Caritas? "Absolutely," Gail says. "Depending on the patient's treatment program, we have patients that go home overnight as a trial discharge; patients that have the same privileges at Villa Caritas that they had at Alberta Hospital Edmonton. It just depends where they are in their treatment."

"One thing I would like to see in your article," says Gail, "is the fact that Villa Caritas is providing an interdisciplinary treatment modality to seniors with psychiatric illness. I think that's a critical point. In a community-integrated model.

"I think that in itself for seniors, our hope in this community, will decrease the fear that some seniors feel about coming to a psychiatric facility for the first time. That happens often. The families would feel that this is a safe place to take their loved ones. And the other thing is that the community at large be aware that this is a short term stay facility and it's an acute facility that is designed to manage psychiatric behaviors in seniors.

"Our hope by being here is to help assist with the stigma that is associated with mental illness at any level. And that's sort of why I've been such a believer since the government announced that this is the right thing to do for the patients."

"The general practitioners are all aware that the Geriatric Psychiatry Program was moving from Alberta Hospital Edmonton to Villa Caritas," says Gail.

"They have to have their family doctor refer them," Joss explains.

Gail nods. "If the patient is appropriate then our consultants will proceed. Our psychiatrists go to see the patient. Each one of our psychiatrists is assigned as a consultant to the acute care hospitals here in Edmonton, the general hospitals, and because we have a referral admission process."

"We are linked with the Crisis Team in the city so if there is an emergency urgent admission, certainly they can contact Villa Caritas. One of our physicians is on call."

"They can go to any Emergency Department in crisis and Emergency Departments do refer to Villa Caritas…if they were requiring our acute psychiatric services they would be admitted here."

"We're working closely with the Geriatric Medicine Team over at the Misericordia. So that will certainly assist our seniors in getting not only the medical expertise that they need but psychiatric expertise."

The sun is streaming through the large windows into the units beyond as we leave. "If people could see how welcoming the setting is and how lovely the care, so people may seek the care because they don't fear the care."

Chapter 10:
Living Accommodations

"Home is not where you live, but where they understand you." —-
Christian Morganstern quotes

"Having moved into his first apartment, our son invited my husband and I for a visit. As we walked in, our son asked if we'd like a cold drink. Mentally patting myself on the back for teaching him to be such a gracious host, I said,"Yes, what do you have?" He walked over to the refrigerator, opened the door, studied the contents, and then replied, "I have pickle juice or water."

Living alone has its challenges and rewards. Isolation and lack of care if needed is a challenge. See Chapter 17 about safety and supervision. But rewards of living alone are the feeling of pride and self-esteem, the ability to make decisions, the smug feeling of competence necessary to rise to the occasion of paying bills, scrubbing one's own floor, even home ownership; yes, Austin, and washing one's own dishes!

Austin Mardon will say he jokingly tells his wife he can't wash dishes because of his medication. But he says that excuse is growing old and stale. He'll have to think of something else soon. They live in a condo they own in a modest area of the city. Home ownership is important to Austin, who has been homeless and lives with a certain fear of homelessness again. He knows no one now can toss him out onto the street. And rental can be difficult if a landlord knows there is a diagnosis of schizophrenia. If a relapse occurs the renter may find herself without a home, perhaps out on the street.

Kenna has lived in the same rented high rise studio suite for six years now. Prior to that she lived for eight years in a charming old house with a woman friend who owned the house, to whom Kenna paid rent. At one time Kenna was a home owner, before the second marriage and also before her divorce in 1987, at which time she shared a house with her second husband. She has no regrets, though. She gained self-respect and independence, and eventual happiness. That's what's in store for those who live alone and love it, like she does.

"Who looks after you?" she has been asked.

Well, nobody. At one time, she was institutionalized. That's who looked after her, nurses, student nurses and the occasional brief visit with a psychiatrist. The social worker was too busy to help her balance her checkbook or find accommodation or settle a costly misunderstanding with Revenue Canada. She did it.

Now she has family and friendship, and children who are independent, caring adults who give back to society; and other people who care, including a competent new psychiatrist, thanks to Forensic Assessment and Community Services (FACS).

She recently saw an RN at the Edmonton Mental Health in the geriatric section - another resource for the older patient (see previous chapter). These are quite recent developments.

She was assessed once by a psychiatrist at the University of Alberta Hospital in the fall of 2009.

Prior to that, her psychiatrist retired many years ago and she was referred to a family physician and the Edmonton Mental Health Clinic. She appeared to fall through the cracks although she took her medications regularly since 1991. A brush with the law in April 2009 provided her the help she needed.

Kenna continues to live on her own, happy in her "castle in the clouds" with no plans to move out or buy her own home. Many schizophrenics can't afford home ownership nor can they obtain a mortgage due to poor credit rating or lack of income.

What are the alternatives?

Some live with parents who become elderly caretakers as they age. Others live with siblings, children, friends or other caretakers. Some are married and have their spouses and families. Some live-in group homes. Some are institutionalized for greater or lesser periods of time. A large percentage are homeless.

We all live in castles in the air at one time or another.

Factors affecting suitable accommodation include cost and social stigma, leading some landlords to refuse housing to the mentally ill. Some affordable areas of the city are unsafe. Those in rural areas may have limited options available for housing or apartment living.

Independent living, home ownership, social stigma, cost of suitable accommodation, perceived inability to care for oneself, and satisfaction in decorating and designing one's very own living space; the independence and joy expressed in Kenna's awkward poem in Chapter One - the card that read, "I hope you enjoy your freedom in your very own place!" Yes, freedom and independence. And happiness – but loneliness at first, too.

Balanced with companionship and security or the stability of someone to look after things? Kenna thinks it's no contest.

The mentally ill face not only stigma but abuse - emotional, physical, sexual and financial abuse from those who profess to care for her or from the public at large. Veiled insults and slights, more open diatribe, neglect, advantages being taken emotionally, physically, sexually, and financially, and the threat of violence. The mentally ill are far more likely to suffer from violence than to inflict it.

They are more likely to be withdrawn and "prefer to be left alone." (source: http://www.schizophrenia.com/poverty.htm) Substance abuse or not taking one's medication, however, does raise the possibility of violence, most often against family members or friends.

The media and entertainment industries unfairly depict the mentally ill as dangerous and brand all with the same iron.

One of the mandates of the Schizophrenia Society of Alberta is to set the media straight in their sometimes very biased and dangerous reporting of the incidence of violence and the possibility for relapse for a "former mental patient". The law is only recently coming abreast of a more humane approach than to put a schizophrenic offender, usually for a minor offense, in jail, but instead ensuring treatment and perhaps community service. (See Chapter 7: The Perception of Violence).

Yes, of course, jail or a psychiatric hospital are also homes for those with schizophrenia.

Iris Court:

The City of Edmonton is building a new assisted living facility in the inner city to house those with schizophrenia who can live on their own. Rents will be affordable and care will be available on-site 24/7. The block of apartments on 93rd Street and 107th Avenue is called Iris Court and will house 21 units including studio suites and 1-bedroom. Residents must be referred by Alberta Health or other partners.

A 2007 study conducted by the Schizophrenia Society of Alberta (SSA) and funded by the Edmonton Joint Planning Committee on Housing entitled "Housing for Persons with Mental Illness: Understanding Their Experiences," revealed:

- The need for affordable housing is a serious concern for people with schizophrenia and other mental illnesses;

- Interviewees reported a reliance on income support such as AISH (Assured Income for the Severely Handicapped), pension, and/or part-time or temporary work. Many reported the amount received from these sources was inadequate to allow for appropriate housing;

- People with schizophrenia want housing support service improved;

- Many would like to see health professionals provide a continuum of services (including housing) that can be individualized according to need, and

- Many voiced the desire for health professionals to encourage skills learning and responsibility in mentally ill persons when possible.

"Households which must spend 30% or more of before-tax income on housing costs are said to be in core housing need.

- AISH (at the time of this study) provides a maximum living allowance of $1,588 per month and an employment income exemption of $400 per month.

- In Edmonton a person with schizophrenia who is solely dependent on AISH is spending over 75% of monthly income on rent."

They go on to say:

Did you know?

- 33% of Canada's homeless are mentally ill;

- 6% of Canada's inmates have schizophrenia;

- 7% of all suicides in Canada are attributed to schizophrenia;

- 50% of people with mental illness in Canada are also challenged by substance abuse.

(source: Iris Court: Addressing the need for affordable housing for those with schizophrenia and other related mental illnesses: Schizophrenia Society of Alberta,
   http://www.schizophrenia.ab.ca/PDFs/2008CaseSupport.pdf) :

Alberta Hospital Edmonton

It's noted that the Province of Alberta planned to close Alberta Hospital Edmonton, a 410-bed psychiatric hospital that houses between 1,650 and 1,700 patients every year. Public outcry, including outcry from psychiatrists, doctors, patients and advocate groups, forced the Province to reconsider. Austin Mardon was one of the advocates who successfully petitioned the Hospital to remain open.

The geriatric program at Alberta Hospital Edmonton had 106 beds and served people with severe mental illnesses over the age of 65. Those persons have now been moved to the facility at Villa Caritas in the west end of Edmonton.

Chapter 11:
Homelessness

"There but for the grace of God go I." —John Bradford

The homeless are an increasing presence in the downtown area of Edmonton where Kenna has lived in her high-rise apartment since 2005. Our mental hospitals tend to turn out the mentally ill onto the street.

It's estimated that 59 percent of the homeless in the United States are schizophrenic (see below). Many homeless persons self-medicate with illicit drugs and alcohol, and panhandling has become a real problem in our communities.

Kenna approaches the street people with compassion and respect. There but for the grace of God... but not all homeless are mentally ill.

Both Mardon and Kenna have adult onset schizophrenia, and as such there is a bond with fellow suffering humanity as they walk to a different drummer down the alleyways of torment and dream. There ought to be a bond amongst all mankind. But sometimes the suffering of others is viewed as none of our business, or worse, their fault. They could pull themselves up by the bootstraps. Right?

Kenna had such an attitude of intolerance and *hubris* (overweening pride) before her devastating slide into schizophrenia and alcoholism. She could have lost everything but she didn't.

She never forgets where she came from, or that she could have ended on a slab in the morgue or rummaging in garbage cans in a back alley. Now, Kenna is surprised she made it this far. She thought she would die early. Many do.

She quit drinking alcoholic beverages completely in 1993 and credits that success with a 12-step program and attendance at fundamentalist churches who encourage sobriety.

She has always been high functioning other than the initial devastation of her "first break" psychosis and the unfortunate period of time in 1990 when she quit taking her medications and became acutely ill once again. She was never homeless and never on AISH. For that she can thank her first husband, who died in 1971 leaving an adequate insurance policy to see his small family through some difficult years ahead. He was never to know of the illness that struck his wife four years later, nor the grim prognosis for so many years.

The first thing Kenna did with the insurance money was buy a modest little house on a corner lot in a working-class neighborhood of Edmonton, where she and the children lived until her second marriage 10 years later.

Mardon was actually homeless and on the street at one time but credits his success to his medications and the support of his wife and father. He and his wife live in a charming little condominium in an unassuming area of Edmonton. He may witness at times a vagrant staggering into an alley, and feel a surge of compassion and guilt that he is warm, safe and cared for, while many others are not. Many are the forgotten and uncared for, the misunderstood, the abused, the tormented.

Austin Mardon, recipient of the Order of Canada in 2006, other awards too numerous to mention here, and the 2010 Medal of Honour from the Alberta Medical Association for his tireless advocacy on behalf of persons challenged with schizophrenia, says, "I've just been out there…many people with schizophrenia for various reasons are afraid of being public…Just being well and being public is advocacy," he says, "and not denying you have the illness. I should be accepted even though I have this disability."

"It's a very difficult road to have the illness," states Austin. "There's a lot of societal discrimination over the years…that I've encountered. Becoming an advocate…in 1993 when I started giving speeches…I didn't intentionally think about it…I thought I have to do something so I started giving speeches and volunteering. I've always been willing to be public about my illness."

Mardon cautions that many individuals with schizophrenia neglect to continue taking their medication and this is the primary reason they become unwell. He talks of society's prejudice, and compares the illness to that of someone in a wheelchair. No one would dream of poking fun at a person in a wheelchair, he says, "but there's a lot of pressure…to remain hidden…"

Not all homeless are mentally ill. Certainly, some mentally ill persons are high functioning like Austin and Kenna. Kenna has never been homeless. But she doesn't know if her experience with a diagnosis of paranoid schizophrenia is different from anyone else's. She knows how difficult she can get, even on regular doses of psychotropic medication, which she takes without fail. Her body chemistry can act up anyhow, causing irritability, impatience or suspicion, but most of the time she's like anyone else; you wouldn't know she has a diagnosis of a serious mental illness. She's one of the few fortunate people in that respect.

Schizophrenia. "Split mind". No, we're not a "split personality". That's a misapprehension. Rather, when we become ill, our thoughts become fragments like confetti sweeping in a windstorm through the tunnels of our tortured brains. We become confused, disoriented, frightened. And very suspicious. The motives of others seem sinister and threatening. We feel threatened. The world is hostile. Our best friends appear to be enemies. We may react with confusion and anger.

Be calm. We won't hurt you. We're a frightened animal at those times. We need medication. Approach us gently, as you would a wounded deer. Realize our physical boundaries may have expanded. Don't attempt to touch us or invade our boundaries. Sometimes even being in the same room with someone else is too confining for us; too close. Threatening. You are dealing with a frightened human being. Be gentle, be calm.

Homeless, unmedicated, the street people medicate themselves with drugs and alcohol, they beg and busk and collect bottles for a living. They talk to themselves. They sleep on park benches and in bus shelters. They wheel their earthly possessions in purloined shopping carts. Some ride bicycles trailed by rough homemade wagons. Some are on pensions for the severely handicapped. Others turn to shoplifting or petty crime.

The majority are harmless. Most are victims themselves, victims of society and of their own naiveté.

Kenna was fortunate. She's able to work. She treasures her university undergraduate degree awarded in 1975. She's had on most occasions an understanding boss. She had friends and family. She had help. Her genes are strong and resilient. She responds well to her medication.

Others are not so privileged. Kenna never forgets where she could have ended up. And she has been down and out, no doubt about it, and she never forgets where she came from, either.

Austin considers himself equally fortunate, but the beast within still stalks him at times in spite of the PhD he has earned, the Antarctic research when he was young, the professional and personal accolades and awards.

We have moments and days, even weeks, of deep anguish and struggle yet, but the cloud has lifted for us; the dragon is off our backs. We try to forget the unkind words. We try to remember and cherish the joys of good health, increasingly more frequent; we hope for the future and endurance for the times that are not so good.

We need understanding and love like anyone else, but more particularly when we are down and out. You will know that by the look in our eyes, by our hunched shoulders; you will recognize that in the vacant stares of the street people and their grateful response to a kind word.

We have learned tolerance and compassion. We don't give up, those of us who have chosen to live and live well, but many of us have low self-esteem. Give us a gentle smile. Give us a helping hand but expect us to help ourselves. We are self-correcting.

Present reality to us in a patient, firm manner and reassure us we are not in danger. Suggest we evaluate the efficacy of our medication. And laugh with us. Most of us have developed a wonderful sense of humor; a sense of the ridiculous and sublime; a sense that we are a jest of God.

We are responsible but not responsible. Therein lies the paradox. Our persona at times of extreme illness may frighten you. Don't be frightened.

I am a wounded deer, looking into a mirror where the wolves of my illness abound within the depths of my eyes. Then the wolves howl once or twice at the surge of the medication through my bloodstream, at a positive caring word from a friend or stranger, and slink back into my brain — now approaching the subconscious, approaching the limits of humanity — where there is a human being in need of understanding and compassion.

Now the wolves are gone and I remain head up and somewhat embarrassed at my behavior; tolerance and love renewed for myself and my friends and family.

- Approximately 200,000 individuals with schizophrenia or manic-depressive illness are homeless, constituting one-third of the approximately 600,000 homeless population (total homeless population statistic based on data from Department of Health and Human Services). These 200,000 individuals comprise more than the entire population of many U.S. cities.

- At any given time, there are more people with untreated severe psychiatric illnesses living on America's streets than are receiving care in hospitals. Approximately 90,000 individuals with schizophrenia or manic-depressive illness are in hospitals receiving treatment for their disease.

Source: Treatment Advocacy Center

We could have been the street person. We sometimes *are* the homeless. We are humanity.

"The Edmonton Committee to End Homelessness is a community-based approach that aims to end homelessness in Edmonton in 10 years.
The committee is made up of leading citizens who represent government, business, labor, healthcare and social services — critical areas that can come together and find solutions to end homelessness." (source: http://www.endedmontonhomelessness.com)
Iris Court is located in the inner city of Edmonton and will open in spring 2011. It is a subsidized 21-unit apartment complex with reasonable rents and 24/7 support to house adults with schizophrenia who are living on low incomes and could otherwise be on the streets. (See Chapter 10: Living Accommodations).

"Approximately 59 percent of people who are currently homeless have a mental illness, and people who have a severe and persistent mental illness like schizophrenia are probably the most vulnerable of that group," says Robin Telasky, spokeswoman for the Schizophrenia Society of Alberta.
(source: http://www.edmontonjournal.com/health/Residence+ schizophrenic+adults+Edmonton+open+spring+2011/2348689/ story.html\#ixzz1DIksboPE)

Chapter 12:
Activities and Hobbies

"He who would learn to fly one day must first learn to stand and walk and run and climb and dance; one cannot fly into flying."—Friedrich Nietzsche

You may think for those with a mental illness that there are special challenges associated with having fun, with finding hobbies you enjoy or work that turns your spindle. You may think that taking classes or attending a gym costs too much and are out of the question for those of us on a fixed income. You may want to take a pottery class but can't afford the clay and firing up a kiln.

Do you smoke? Do you drink? Do you eat too much fast food and unhealthy restaurant meals? Quit that. Put the money into a glass jar and save it for a few months.

Then take that pottery course or go golfing this summer. Rent the clubs. Find a ride out there. Carry your own bags. If you're on AISH or a pension you may find a gym is paid for. If it's not, make your own home gym. Do you have a DVD player? Rent some exercise DVDs from your public library and take them home and watch them. Use the ones you like, bring them back, take out some more. Look on the tables at Zellers or Wal-Mart for exercise DVDs for five or six dollars. Walk. Get a pedometer from someplace free if you can. Go to parks. Swim. The cost may be covered by your AISH. Check with the city for that.

Bus fare is reasonable if you're on AISH. Take the bus to unexplored areas. Take out books from your public library. Membership is free if you can't afford it. Walk and take the bus. We do.

If you don't smoke, if you don't drink or take illicit drugs, if you don't go out several times a week to restaurants for unhealthy foods, if you don't spend your money on unhealthy groceries - if you own a computer look up Hillbilly Housewife. She has loads of money saving recipes and ideas for us. Free. Look up Fly Lady. She'll help you keep your house clean and tidy and you can purge your closets.

Go to a thrift store or consignment shop for household effects and neat clothing. Buy retro clothing if you like that, or bright colors, something that fits and is clean and trendy. And cheap. Gently used. Find your own style. Look at fashion magazines in the library or on-line fashion sites.

You can use the library computers, you know - go on-line there. Do some research. Find hobbies that don't cost a lot. Or save and splurge maybe in the dead of our cold dark winters, grow flowers indoors or go to the Muttart Conservatory and have an hour in the desert and next hour in the tropics. Spend a day during the Easter season there when they have a special exhibit, or at Christmastime or Valentine's Day with a special someone or a good friend.

Don't spend a lot on gifts. Be creative. Make your own cards. Learn to draw or paint. Write poems. Write little stories. Write your memoirs. Don't expect to make a living that way. Do it for fun. Give them to friends and family members as gifts.

Bake cookies and healthy muffins. Give them as gifts to the poor. Those poorer than you. Invite someone over. Buy two pretty mismatched English bone china teacups at the thrift store and entertain. Try a new vegetable. Smile at a child. Talk to a homeless person unless you're homeless yourself, and then smile at the next person who comes by your corner. So what if he doesn't smile back? Eventually someone will.

Learn to sing and dance. Then learn to fly.

Maybe you've always wanted to travel. Can you accompany someone as a companion? Would that be something you're competent to do or like to do? Or take a day trip now and then out of town. If you live in a rural area then go to town. Enjoy the day. Carpe diem. Offer to barter something you can do like drive part of the way with a friend.

Find cheaper accommodation or subsidized housing.

Find a church. The Salvation Army is excellent. Find a large Catholic basilica if you're Roman Catholic. If you're Ukrainian or Greek Catholic find that. If you're Jewish find a temple. If you're Islam find a mosque. Worship in the ways of your fathers and mothers, or worship in a new way. Be a pagan. Be a free spirit and create your own religion but don't be a Messiah. Meditate. Buy or find some candles and light them. Get some incense but be careful of fire and smoke. It may irritate your allergies and you may set fire to the settee.

Take a nap. But not too long. Find the right medication. Ask until you get it right. Insist on a proper therapist, one who understands you and likes you.

If you need an aid to help with household chores, yard work or walking check out Aids to Daily Living if you're physically disabled. If you need aides then check it out with a social worker or occupational therapist. Talk to the nurses. They know a lot. Ask your doctor to write you a referral for a Handicapped Sticker if you need one.

Write poetry. Tell clean jokes. Write your memories and make a booklet of them with photographs. If you have a camera take lots of pictures. Take pictures of your city or rural area. Take pictures of the elderly with their wise eyes. Take pictures of yourself in all your different guises. Make a scrapbook. Sew your own gaudy curtains. Take classes on-line or go to the library and learn how to do things. Learn how to make things inexpensively. If you have money travel a bit.

Get a job or volunteer. Get a part-time job in a used book store. Get a part time job at Goodwill and go through the neat clothing that comes in first, before anyone else gets it, pick out what looks good on you.

Read the fashion headlines and the magazines in doctors' offices. Get your hair cut at an inexpensive hairdresser who's good and who knows what you like and what looks good on you. Look around until you find someone you like and who understands what you're looking for. Get a haircut for $15 and keep it trimmed yourself. Then go back and give them a tip. Give them a dollar.

Get a coffee at McDonald's for 80 cents if you're a senior. Or a coffee and muffin for $1.30. It's cheap and the coffee there is good.

Get a double cheeseburger for $1.69 at McDonald's. It's big enough for a fast food meal. I think it's 360 calories for that cheeseburger. Don't get a Big Mac. Don't get fries. And make that a treat. Don't go to a restaurant to eat more than once a month. Better still, get a salad. But a salad is more expensive at McDonald's than a cheeseburger, you know.

Make your own salads. Get a big head of lettuce, some celery, some Trail Mix, a tomato or green pepper, any other kind of vegetable or an orange or apple, and make a nice salad with some dressing you bought in a small jar from Wal-Mart. Eat it with some Melba toast. Make your own individual sized pizza with tortillas or pitas piled with veggies, tomatoes and a piece of cheese, and broiled or baked for a few minutes.

Buy a big bag of oatmeal and cook some in the microwave. Put 1/3 cup of dry oatmeal in a mug and add water or milk, cinnamon and raisins or fruit. Nuke it for 2 minutes and add milk, honey or brown sugar.

Buy some regular popcorn and cook it in the microwave in a brown paper bag. Don't buy the little bags of butter flavor popcorn. Pop your own and add your own flavorings. Spray it with oil and salt it if you must. Have a treat while you watch that movie you got from the library.

Learn to play a musical instrument if Uncle Bob left you a banjo or his old keyboard. Take lessons on-line or buy a book from a used bookstore. It doesn't matter if you're not that good. Don't play too loud late at night if you live in an apartment, though. Play in the park in the summertime or busk with a license. Sing. Learn some Christmas carols and volunteer with a church group to go caroling.

Try to find an old bike you can afford or see if someone would give you a bicycle. Paint it orange. Ride it everywhere but be careful in traffic. Kenna has a lovely bicycle but she isn't comfortable riding it. She bought a stationary bike at a thrift shop for $25 and uses that. Someday she'll be more confident to ride her regular bicycle on a bike trail.

Investigate the parks in town. Have a picnic every weekend in summer. See the fireworks on July 1st or July 4th if you're American. If you're English celebrate Guy Fawkes Day. Celebrate all the holidays. It doesn't have to be expensive.

There are places to go in the squares downtown or at other venues throughout the city. Take advantage of free barbecues and breakfasts offered by political leaders and community leagues and churches. Vote for them. Join clubs that don't have expensive fees or will waive their fees. If you're on AISH you can get a free membership to a city recreation center including swimming pool, hot tubs, sauna and gym.

Be an armchair traveler. Watch documentaries of foreign places and keep up on the news. Talk about it. It'll make you more interesting. It's not all about us, you know. If you own a computer, Netflix streaming is great for movies for $7.99 a month in Canada.

Learn a new trade. Sometimes for nothing. Sometimes on grants or for research. Get involved. Work at something new. Do something else if you don't like it. Read inspirational and motivational stories. Read biographies of great men and women.

Have a slogan. "*Strong Women Stay Young*" for example, the name of a book. It's physical fitness; lifting weights.

Do you have a specific interest? Yes? Then follow it; ferret out its mysteries and secrets. No specific interests? Find one! The world is full of possibilities. Talk to people. Not about you. About them.

Write a story. Write a journal. Press flowers in a book. Make your own sachets and potpourri. Put some lavender under your pillow to treat a headache and make you sleep better.

Track your dreams. Find out what your dreams mean. Talk about them to someone if they don't embarrass you. Take a hot or cold shower or a bubble bath with floating candles.

Be free. Have fun. But be responsible. Grow and mature and don't worry what other people say about you. It's none of your business what other people think about you. You're important and you're unique.

Join a neighborhood softball game. Toss around a Frisbee in the park. Get a cat or dog or goldfish or plant. Get a cactus. They don't need much water but they need a lot of sun. Collect little colored interesting stones, rocks and driftwood. Decorate your plants with them. Put up a flag but not on your window. Display it proudly. We live in a great country.

Canada is the second largest country by area in the world next to Russia. Do you know anything about the rest of our country? The territories? The Inuit, the First Nations?

Do you need a 12 Step program? If you think you have an addiction problem, find a phone and call them. They're in the phone book. Go to a meeting every day for 90 days. Or start a group or head up a group if you can't find what you like.

Join a hiking club or create your own with a couple of friends. Get a fanny pack or a back pack and carry a bottle of water and a sandwich. Make sure the bottle is attractive. Get a hiking stick and decorate it with bells or feathers.

Wear a baseball cap or straw hat in summer and a warm hat in winter. Make sure they're clean and funky, or conservative if that's your style. Develop your own unique sense of style. Don't let anyone else tell you how to dress. Not even me.

If you need reading glasses get a pair at the drug store. Save up for the best pair you can afford and buy a nice-looking pair with a case. It'll be like magic. You can read. You can watch TV. You can surf the net.

What's a three-letter word for something you surf? A mature friend said "sea" and the answer was "web". Times have changed. Don't get reading glasses at a dollar store. You'll ruin your eyes and you won't be able to see all that well anyhow. Save and get a better pair.

It's important to share activities with friends or family. It'll bring you closer unless you fight about it! Find family activities you all enjoy, including the children. It could be something as simple as making muffins together, or a walk in the park, or a day at the Museum or the flower Conservatory. You could make paper flowers or homemade paper. Read the magazines at the library and find ideas.

It's a big world.

Find things for your idle hands to do. And if you're too busy already, then slow down! Say no. Delegate. Prioritize. Organize. Get your priorities straight. Stress can be positive, but too much will kill you. Stop worrying so dang much. See the lilies of the field how they're clothed and even Solomon in his splendor wasn't dressed that fine. See the sparrow how God looks after it. But note they do their jobs.

See the grasshopper and the ant, the ant busy; the grasshopper playing. Which is wiser? The grasshopper will die when winter comes but the ant will survive underground with his provisions for spring. All have their own time. Who's right? Certainly, I'm not always right.

Is the grasshopper right? A brief flame dying quickly in the night sky. Or a long slow burn to the end of an era. You choose. That's what's meant by freedom. It's a choice, and opportunity does knock more than once. Just listen at that door and He'll come again. Treat yourself well. You are a worthy, important part of the world. Act accordingly. Learn to love yourself.

See what you can do to find a fine balance. Too little stress and you're a couch potato. Too much stress and you're fried. A certain amount of stress is necessary. "Positive stress moves us toward goal achievement. Negative stress saps us of energy." (source: http://www.about-goal-setting.com/goal-setting-success-guide/27-positive-stress.html)

Maybe both were right; the grasshopper should marry the ant. Do what you love. And don't hurt anybody.

I remember the story of a man who had an abusive boss. Years later the man was talking to a former colleague who asked him what he could have done about the situation, expecting the fellow to say he could have gone to the union or he could have quit. Instead, the man said, "I could have laughed."

I think of a quote from Voltaire who said he prayed that God would make his enemies ridiculous. And his prayer was answered.

Chapter 13:
The Role of Stress

"You can't outsmart crazy."—Jon Stewart

We can all recognize stress in our lives. We usually think it's a bad thing. Stress is defined by medical doctors as an organism's response to environmental pressures or tensions, which can result in physical or emotional symptoms. Long term stress can result in high blood pressure, heart attack, stroke or even cancer. (Source: http://medical-dictionary.thefreedictionary.com/stress) Emotional symptoms may include anxiety and other psychiatric symptoms. Examples of stressors include the news on TV, the threat of terrorism since 2001, war time experiences or a demanding job.

It's been postulated that stress alone accounts for a large percentage of physical illnesses in North America today. Physical modalities such as yoga and tai chi are becoming accepted now for relief of stress rather than viewed as a counterculture as they were at one time. There's better acceptance of alternative therapies now than in a previous generation, and this includes by medical doctors and therapists as well as the public in general. Stress can indeed lead to violence or self-harm, or depression and anxiety symptoms. However, there's an upside to stress.

We all need a certain amount of stress in our lives in order to function. "Complete prevention of stress is neither possible nor desirable, because stress is an important stimulus of human growth and creativity, as well as an inevitable part of life." (source: http://medical-dictionary.thefreedictionary.com/stress)

Without stress, we might be all armchair French Fries, lolling around all day in our housecoats contemplating our navels with no reason to get "up and at 'em, guards", as Kenna's mother used to say. We need incentive. Although personalities differ and physical and mental capacities vary in each individual, still some individuals handle stress better than others, but all need their level of internal prodding to produce their best efforts. This might be called stress.

A doctor's perspective would be different than an herbalist's, for example. The medical model historically dealt primarily with physical effects such as blood pressure and heart disease, the effects of chronic anxiety on a person's body. Burnout is common in nurses who deal with those who are terminally ill, or with hospice patients, as their patients will eventually die and their efforts to keep their patient comfortable may not be possible. Stress implies a lack of control.

Is there a way to reframe stress? You will recall from Chapter 4 we talked of "reframing", or changing our perspective of a situation or "frame" to a different and more positive outlook or meaning.

Kenna attended a seminar on CBT wherein the presenters drew a diagram on a whiteboard of a large triangle with equal sides. On the bottom arm of the triangle a presenter wrote "behavior"; on the left arm she wrote "thoughts"; and on the right arm of the triangle she wrote "feelings". The presenters, associated with the Mental Health & Addictions Clinic in Edmonton, Alberta, commented that changing any one of these will change the others.

In particular, one cannot change her feelings or emotions. Feelings or emotions must be changed by changing thoughts or behavior. Thoughts are more difficult to change but it can be done with perseverance. The easiest way to change one's emotions is through changing the behavior, and that's apparently the premise of CBT.

The presenters commented that stress has a role in this, both positive and negative. We all need a certain amount of stress in our lives, but when our psychic pot is filled to overflowing with stressors such as loss of job or work stress, financial stress, interpersonal stress and so on, then it overflows with the results of stress such as physical, emotional or mental illnesses. We may fall ill with a cold or a more serious acute or chronic illness. We may have a relapse if we are persons with a mental illness such as schizophrenia.

The therapist asked the question, "What can we do to relieve the stress?" She drew a diagram of a vessel overflowing from a dripping tap, and with a spigot on the bottom to relieve the pressure that otherwise would eventually flow over the top of the vessel. There were several suggestions from the floor. I know you can come up with many yourself.

Someone suggested yoga or tai chi. Walking is very beneficial, or any form of physical exercise which induces "feel good" endorphins and leads to a feeling of well-being hours or even days after the exertion.

Try watching a funny movie, reading a funny book or story, talking to a good friend, calling a therapist; someone even suggested cleaning house! Try "Retail therapy" - shopping if one's finances can afford it - perhaps getting some new clothes or a power tool.

Go to a thrift shop or consignment store. Just "window shopping" was suggested by someone. Looking in the stores at pretty things or new cars or something that one perhaps can't afford to buy but one can dream, can't they?

Going mall walking. Go to a good movie or meet a friend for coffee.

There were many suggestions as ways to take that pressure off. Someone else suggested medication or talking to a doctor. There are all kinds of personalities and all kinds of people who react differently to the same stressors. Choose what suits you best. Some people like to journal or write poetry. Others play music or play a musical instrument themselves and/or sang. You don't have to be the best. Just enjoy yourself.

Kenna likes to go for a walk and end up at a bistro for a cup of coffee or herbal tea. Austin talks to his wife; perhaps goes out for a coffee or the infrequent hot chocolate for relaxation and to get out of the apartment. Others suggested hobbies such as needlework, quilting or scrapbooking; working on cars or woodworking. See the chapter on "fun" and hobbies.

Positive Stress

Sure, we all need a certain amount of stress in our lives and there is positive stress. (source: http://www.stressfocus.com/stress_focus_-article/positive-and-negative-stress.htm).

This positive stress response involves something as simple as putting on a sweater when we're cold (reacting to a situation to change it for the better) or the classic "fight or flight" situation when stress may help us to escape from danger.

Of course, the "fight or flight" responses may become chronic in nature due perhaps to postmodern life stressors which were not present a couple of generations ago. That's when psychological distress and physical illnesses can arise.

But the creative juices can start to flow when exposed to a moderate level of stress, such as an artist composing a painting in response to the pressure of the creative impulse, a new scientific or technological discovery, or a student facing an exam.

If a student feels no stress when writing an exam he may be too "laid back" to do his best or to recall facts or skills that must be used in the successful completion of the exam. If he is too stressed then he might experience a "block," however.

Positive and negative stress can affect different individuals in different ways, just as early childhood can affect different personalities differently.

Positive stress can help us to solve problems. It can also lead to a sense of wellbeing or even euphoria after completing a task. This is in contrast to negative stress, which is the type of stress most commonly thought of when stress is mentioned. Negative stress, however, can cause many adverse effects.

Negative Stress

Negative stress is what we commonly think of when stress or stressors are mentioned. And we want to avoid stress! Well, no one can completely avoid stress and it wouldn't be beneficial for us to do so. There *are* positive effects (see above).

But in the postmodern world stress has become almost endemic, whether it's in the workplace, as a result of watching daily news on television, terrorism, warfare, financial strain or bullying in school and other sources of distress. Yes, this is when stress might be synonymous with "distress".

Negative stress is sometimes identified as Type 1: stress reversible by oneself; and Type 2: stress reversible by others. Note that in all cases the stress is considered reversible, or capable of being fixed, either by ourselves or with help.

Some examples of stress reducing interventions are listed above under CBT. These might include walking or other forms of exercise in the case of Type 1 (reversible by ourselves), watching a funny movie or reading a funny book, taking a bubble bath or aromatherapy and so on. Examples of interventions that are needed for Type 2 stress (reversible by others) might include calling a good friend or therapist or enlisting family members or community workers to help.

The good news in all this is that negative stress is reversible, according to many sources. As it's commonly a reaction to events in the environment, then changing the environment might indicate a positive reaction to stress, such as when one finds a new job after being fired. Perhaps a better job (reframing?).

Chronic negative stress, perhaps even from childhood, has been blamed for physical illnesses as disparate as irritable bowel syndrome, asthma, heart disease, diabetes and arthritis. But a word of caution. Don't blame yourself and don't blame your family and friends. That can only be counterproductive.

Change your environment if you must - if you're itchy then scratch the itch; if you're warm take off a sweater; if you're cold put on warm clothes. But blame is not going to make it better. Rather, take responsibility for what you can do, and if you can't do it yourself, then enlist competent help. Remember the Serenity Prayer often quoted in 12 Step meetings:

> *God grant me the serenity*
> *to accept the things I cannot change,*
> *courage to change the things I can*
> *And wisdom to know the difference.*

There are negative methods people employ to attempt to reduce stress such as smoking, substance abuse, over eating, excessive exercise, bulimia, sleeping too much or too little, or violence. These are obviously counterproductive and even harmful.

Chapter 14:
Medications

"We'll drink a drink a drink to Lily the Pink...she invented medicinal compounds...most efficacious in every case." —The Irish Rovers

Medications are possibly the single most important high powered rifles in the arsenal of weapons against this insidious yet sometimes suddenly explosive disease called schizophrenia. Much has changed in the past 60 years since Austin's grandmother was forced to struggle on her own, and in the 30 years since Kenna was given "major tranquilizers" like chlorpromazine in massive doses which was like being hit over the head with a stone.

Today we have antipsychotics and the new generation of psychotropic medications with milder side effects, faster response times and less cost. And more research is being done now than in those early days when mental illness was the poor sister of the pharmaceutical companies. Even today, however, research on medications for the mentally ill is marginal when compared with other physical diseases which frequently employ celebrities and high profile media coverage to call attention to their fund raising efforts and public awareness.

There's nothing wrong with that, and they are meaningful organizations and charities, but the stigma of schizophrenia, bipolar and other mental illnesses remains embedded in the public consciousness even today. A generation ago "cancer" was a taboo word. Today it seems that "schizophrenia," "depression" or "bipolar" are equally taboo. There's hope for the future, though, and the modern generation of medications are very much a part of it.

Medications work very well to control the symptoms of schizophrenia but they can have severe side effects. It's important not to stop taking your medications without consulting your doctor, who can help find a medication that you can tolerate and that works well for you.

WebMD has the following to say about the different kinds of medications available to treat schizophrenia. It's noted that often more than one medication is used in conjunction with perhaps two or three others.

"Medicines used most often to treat schizophrenia include:
- First-generation antipsychotics, such as haloperidol (Haldol), perphenazine, and chlorpromazine. They are used to reduce anxiety and agitation and to stop delusions and hallucinations. These medicines can work very well but often have severe side effects, such as tardive dyskinesia, which causes uncontrolled body movements.

- Second-generation antipsychotics, such as risperidone (Risperdal), paliperidone (Invega), olanzapine (Zyprexa), ziprasidone (Geodon), and quetiapine (Seroquel). These medicines effectively treat symptoms of schizophrenia and may help reduce the risk of relapse.

- Clozapine, such as Clozaril. This medicine is approved in the United States for treating severe schizophrenia that has not improved with other treatment and for suicidal behavior caused by schizophrenia. In the U.S., your doctor needs special permission to prescribe clozapine for treating schizophrenia. You may need checkups as often as once a week if you take clozapine.

"The following medicines often are used along with antipsychotic medicines and clozapine:

- Lithium carbonate, such as Lithobid and Eskalith. This medicine regulates moods. You will need your blood tested every week when you first start taking it and every 6 or 12 months after you know the correct dose. These tests check the levels of lithium carbonate in your blood, because too much can be dangerous.

- Antianxiety medicines, such as clonazepam (Klonopin) and diazepam (for example, Valium). These medicines reduce anxiety and nervousness.

- Anticonvulsant medicines, such as carbamazepine (for example, Tegretol) and valproate (for example, Depakote). These medicines can keep your mood stable and reduce symptoms during a relapse.

- Antidepressant medicines, such as selective serotonin reuptake inhibitors (SSRIs) (for example, Zoloft or Celexa) or tricyclic antidepressants (for example, Pamelor). These medicines reduce symptoms of depression that often occur along with schizophrenia."

A couple of poems by Kenna:

Pamelor oh Pamelor
How you make my feelings soar
How I love Nortriptyline
On which my psych is rather keen
But there is nothing better for
Bipolar folks than Pamelor.

Oh, Ritalin sky
All cream and grey and cozy
Sun coming up

On my subconscious rosy
Peach-colored thoughts
Heart like lambskin leather
Oh, Ritalin sky
How you've changed the weather!

Here it might be added that we've met people with bipolar illness who appeared to share many of the traits of schizophrenia. This can lead to misdiagnose, sometimes for several years, and resultant incorrect treatment.

"I was diagnosed at various times with manic-depressive illness (bipolar) and later schizoaffective," says Kenna, "and as a result the medications I was given didn't help particularly well to relieve my symptoms of paranoia, delusions and hallucinations."

The manager of a professional institution with which we are both familiar is bipolar and a delightful fellow he is, with compassion and empathy for all who enter the doors. Kenna had a friend once who maintained she was bipolar although she failed to exhibit many of the symptoms of mania alternating with depression that typically characterizes this diagnosis. Her medication is perhaps, as a result, incorrect.

The former friend is a talented artist born in another country and with a different culture. We can imagine all sorts of us dancing around the Maypole of life, caroling loudly in our respective languages, like the tower of Babel:

Première ronde :
Ah ! Mon beau château !
Ma tant', tire, lire, lire ;
Ah ! Mon beau château !
Ma tant', tire, lire, lo.

Deuxième ronde :
Le nôtre est plus beau,

Ma tant', tire, lire, lire ;
Le nôtre est plus beau,
Ma tant', tire, lire, lo.

This is just to say that depression often accompanies schizophrenia and may occur as a coating on top of the paranoia, delusions and hallucinations; depression may compound the chances of a misdiagnosis or layer another diagnosis of mental illness on the original illness of schizophrenia. This seems common enough.

Chapter 15:
Mentoring

"Do not wait for leaders; do it alone, person to person." - Mother Teresa

Kenna called SZ Magazine to order more copies of the Summer 2010 issue as she had an article published there. And the founder and CEO, Bill MacPhee, answered the phone. Diagnosed with schizophrenia in March 1994, Bill MacPhee subsequently founded *Magpie Publishing Inc.* and *SZ Magazine.* He has received numerous awards for his advocacy, consulting and counseling on behalf of those suffering from schizophrenia. Bill speaks widely on the subject of schizophrenia—Kenna was thrilled to talk to this icon—briefly, it is true, but he took her information and would send her magazines. She told him, ending her call, that she never had a lot of role models.

"My role models were pirates and villains gleaned from books, movies, and songs. Now there are real life heroes, flawed and funny and falling down on their faces into cream pies thrown by life itself, getting up and laughing and crying rivers of tears — hugging me and loving me and allowing me to love in return. Thank you, friends and renewed family.

Yes, I fell out of the boat. Oops, here the water's fine. The shore is silver sand and I see a Blue Lagoon. Who needs a boat? Even my wonderful children, new friends and renewed family are here to meet me."

Well, sometimes even an inner tube would have done. Or a life raft. Any port in a storm they say, and the storms can overwhelm us without a rudder and a good captain at the helm.

"A mentor is someone who allows you to see the hope inside yourself." (Oprah Winfrey). See the previous chapters on Austin's mentoring and the role of the SSA.

Chapter 16:
Safety and Supervision

"Home is not where you live, but where they understand you."
—Christian Morganstern

Living Independently

Kenna's rough verses in Chapter 1 reveal just how significant a home of her own was to her after months of living in a psychiatric ward surrounded by strangers.

"A room of one's own," said Woolf. She was right. I did not understand before...

She owned her own house and then a townhouse condo in north Edmonton before marrying in 1982. She relinquished rights to the matrimonial home in exchange for a speedy and welcome divorce in 1987. Since that time, she has rented. Kenna prefers to rent rather than have the responsibility and expense of home ownership at this time.

Austin, after experiencing homelessness on the streets of Edmonton, has purchased his own condominium in a modest area of the city so that no one can ever put him out onto the street again. The condominium is paid for, and Austin and his wife live in the knowledge they are secure in their own home.

"Behold I stand at the door and knock, if anyone hears my voice and opens the door, I will come into him and dine with him and he with me…" (Rev. 3:20, Holy Bible KJV)

Very hospitable, Austin and Catherine Mardon open their doors to friends as well as strangers. On Christmas Eve and again on New Year's Eve they host a party for a number of disparate people who otherwise might have nowhere to go.

It's important for those with limited income and perhaps limited mobility to live in an area close to public transport or within walking distance of grocery stores, thrift shops, banks, restaurants and stores that provide amenities. That's the reason many of the mentally ill choose to live in certain areas of the city, as well as the more inexpensive areas of the city. Their choice is not only due to financial concerns.

There are pitfalls to taking on a mortgage for those who can't afford the payments or have frequent hospitalizations, and it's difficult if not almost impossible to find a mortgage if someone is living on a limited income such as AISH. If private funding can't be found then renting or living with parents or siblings is the best option.

No credit or a bad credit rating, a criminal record, social isolation, ostracism because of a diagnosis of a mental illness, all must be taken into account before being able to rent or own in a safer area with a better quality of life. My advice has always been to live in the best area one can afford, but that's not always possible due to the above circumstances.

There's also a safety concern with equipment such as stoves which may be turned on and forgotten, or equipment such as access to coat hooks or knives in an institutional setting, which may be self-harm hazards.

Caregiving

The caretaking kind of role that was encouraged in the past was thought necessary primarily because of recurrence of symptoms or the attitude that we're not able to look after ourselves, the dangers of mental illness recurring or our actions becoming unsafe to ourselves or others. There's the possibility of self-harm or suicide.

The suicide rate in people who have been diagnosed with schizophrenia is high. I heard at one time that 1 out of 13 of us die from suicide. What would prevent that? Less social isolation? Are auditory hallucinations telling us to harm ourselves or others, making supervision in group homes such as halfway houses, Iris Court or Villa Caritas sometimes necessary?

There are concerns of safety on the job for those who work outside the home, safety at home, safety in social interactions. It's important to protect oneself as well as others, as schizophrenic individuals are often victims of violence, not the other way around. They often do violence to themselves through suicide attempts or self-harm; the homeless mentally ill are often at the mercy of those stronger, at the mercy of those who would abuse them, at the mercy of the law.

Emotional and psychological violence sometimes are inflicted on the mentally ill by families, acquaintances and therapists, particularly in the past, as has been suggested throughout this book. Some have been protected by well-meaning families and friends; others have been cast out and isolated.

Kenna and Austin don't mean to point fingers nor do they mean to ostracize those who care for their loved ones who are mentally ill, but statistically it is true that individuals with schizophrenia are much more likely to be victims of violence than to inflict violence, and society at large doesn't realize this.

For those who have caregivers such as parents, there are concerns such as what happens when the aging caregiver dies or is no longer able to give care. Legal considerations are important to consider such as guardianship, living wills, delegating alternative caregivers, the role of aging caregivers and the aging or senior person who has lived with a diagnosis of mental illness for most of their adult lives.

There's a wonderful documentary created by a woman named Bonnie Shaw Klein from Vancouver, BC, who is a film maker. The documentary is called *Shameless - The Art of Disability* and is a National Film Board film.

Poignant, funny, insightful, intelligent and inspirational, the film documents a group of persons with physical and mental disabilities who have risen above society's expectations of them. There's a physically challenged man who's a standup comedian, for example, and an artist with a mental disability; as well as Bonnie Shaw Klein herself, who suffered a stroke at a young age and has created this kaleidoscope of hope.

You'll find books and articles that portray us as burdens. You'll find people in all walks of life who brand us with the stigma of the "Scarlet 'S'" on our foreheads, as Austin states at times. There are individuals in our own circle of friends who are jealous of our successes.

Don't take our independence and freedom from us. But we tend to be vulnerable members of society as well, often victimized and misunderstood. Though we are vulnerable, don't forget we are also valuable. Ask us what we want. Ask us what we need. In the words of The Elephant Man, "I am a human being."

Chapter 17:
Finding joy and meaning while living with schizophrenia

"Joy is not in things; it is in us."—Richard Wagner

At one time in the late 1980s Kenna was hospitalized in a ward at Alberta Hospital Edmonton where there was a young woman who spoke English as a foreign language. Her family came every day and combed her hair, brought her ethnic foods, looked after her needs, brought her new clothing, and provided companionship. Was this the culture from which she had emerged as a new immigrant to Canada or was it simply a caring family?

Listing goals, planning what is possible and what is not, finding examples of successful and happy people with schizophrenia, are all important methods of instilling hope in the struggling individual who may feel that her life is over, due to a diagnosis of mental illness.

A therapist commented to Kenna recently that a person with mental illness can have a loving and stable relationship with another who doesn't have a mental illness, and why not think so well of oneself that it doesn't really make a difference?

A movie was popular a few years ago called "A Beautiful Mind", a story based on the factual story of a brilliant mathematician named John Nash, a Nobel Laureate recipient in Economics. Some people don't understand even now that John Nash has schizophrenia and that the movie is not simply a fantasy or based on imagination. Insights into the brain that is not functioning well are rare and understanding is even rarer.

Mental illness doesn't mean we are stupid or that we cannot function in society. It's important to live well, and as someone said once, living well is the best revenge. Anything is possible.

We studied Maslow's Hierarchy of Needs at post-secondary schools and his concept of self-actualization after the basic physical needs are met. There should be no barriers to that.

In the early 1980s Kenna's psychiatrist told her that self-actualization was impossible for her and she should be satisfied with "coping". A fighter, she didn't accept that prognosis and found joy and meaning in life even in the midst of anguish at the time.

It's difficult to speculate what brings about hope and motivation. If hope and motivation could only be bottled and sold in pill form! But hope and motivation exist and sometimes take the form of spirituality, a church fellowship or place of worship, or private communion with a higher power or what we sometimes call God. Spirituality can be a means of comfort and companionship.

There's a negative side to optimism, which may cause a manic or hyper-excited state, or unrealistic expectations or dreams. There's a negative side to spirituality, and some churches have unwittingly harmed their members by participating in exorcisms or encouraging members in religious delusions.

It's difficult to draw the line, as religious delusions are fairly common. We'll leave this to your individual conscience and would only caution that one should check with trusted people and sources before embarking on a course that seems delusional or fantastic.

Certainly, joy and meaning in life is possible. Sometimes all around us others seem to be living "lives of quiet desperation." We tend to misread social cues; we tend to be careless of personal hygiene; we tend to be distracted at times as our voices murmur in our ears or our visions sometimes beatifically conjure us.

But we refuse to be victims. We must stand up and enjoy the rights everyone else enjoys.

We see contentment but frustration, too. We see anger and defeat in "normal" people. We see unhappiness on the golf courses and the universities and trade centers of the world. We could maybe teach them a thing or two, about a simpler life, simple joys and the discovery of ourselves at the end of it all.

Chapter 18:
Final thoughts

"I feel like a tiny bird with a big song!"—Jerry Van Amerongen

The purpose of writing this book was to help our fellow travelers to understand and accept themselves and the diagnosis of that "Scarlet 'S' " - schizophrenia, and to encourage those interested in assisting us on our journey. Thus includes those who would help and understand us: the medical personnel, the physicians, the therapists, the counselors, the nurses, the families, parents, landlords, employers, significant others, and friends.

Did we accomplish our purpose? What's the future for schizophrenia and ourselves? It's been a long journey and this book has helped us chronicle *our* stories, *our* battles, *our* successes, strengths and weaknesses.

You have your own. We'd like to hear about *your* joys and despairs. Try journaling and sharing your joys and despairs, those of you who partake in our struggle.

Seek out the resources listed in the back of this book. Join a group you're interested in, or something that you've never thought of as an interest that could turn into a fascinating hobby or even a job. Learn a new skill. Start small and remember KIS - Keep it Simple.

We have minds that can become easily overloaded, especially if stressed, so be aware. It's possible to live out our lives with health, companionship, and happiness. Austin was told once he would die young as a result of his medications. Kenna was told she would be in and out of hospitals for the rest of her life, would not be able to work, and she had difficulty obtaining insurance.

Chemical dependence is often a challenge for those who try to self-medicate themselves with alcohol or other drugs. Some of us smoke too much, eat too much, or drink too much coffee. We're all part of the human race and we all must respect ourselves, our bodies and minds enough to view them as temples.

Be happy for your friends when good fortune pats them on the back. Someone said once if they saw the universe laid out in all its splendor before them and all the beauty and wonder of the world within their hands, still it would be meaningless if they were alone.

I'm not talking about dating or marriage or a significant other. Love yourself, gather positive and supportive people around you, and it will all come together.

Pet therapy is real. Someone once said if you can look after a pet you can look after yourself. Be sure you can look after that special cat, dog, bird, or fish and you may find they're your best friend at times. Plants are a good thing. Remember to water and feed them, too.

Make your living space beautiful, no matter how small and no matter how humble. Walk and swim and hike and lift weights. If you're on AISH you'll get a free pass to a City Recreation Centre: use it! Exercise will pump out those endorphins that make you feel so good.

Take a walk in the park. Listen to your doctor or therapist. Clean up and dress up. You can choose nice clothes from a thrift shop or you can choose ratty old t-shirts and jeans. You can eat McDonald's fries and burgers or you can buy your own groceries and learn to cook healthy. Put your food in individual size containers and freeze it. Make your own TV dinners.

Ask your friends to come help you clean your house and supply them with iced tea, homemade pizza and a lot of laughs. Homemade pizza? Get some pitas or soft tortillas, brush them with tomato paste, sprinkle on some cheese and vegetables and a bit of meat, and sauté in a frying pan until the cheese melts and the pita is brown.

Find a recipe book you can follow. Can't cook? Learn to cook.

Can't clean? Do it or ask for help.

Not perfect? Admit it. Your friends and family aren't perfect either.

Find your own spirituality. Be honest and look for the truth and the good in every person you meet and every situation. It's your choice.

Be happy.

Resources

Depending on which province/state or country in which you live, resources for mental illness will vary. It's very useful to contact the mental health association in your area such as the Canadian Mental Health Association or the Schizophrenia Society of Canada.

Check out free courses, advice, reading materials, and groups offered by your local mental health organizations or public library. You may use a computer at your local library for the cost of a library card (which could be free).

Learn to utilize the internet and email if you have a computer or access to one. You might enjoy games or on-line conversations with friends or you may find computer games enjoyable. There are many resources offered on-line and the internet makes research easy—but be aware that not everything you find on-line is true, and not all your on-line contacts are trustworthy.

Look for subsidized housing, find crisis line numbers and use them if necessary, check out subsidized or free legal services such as Legal Aid or Students' Legal Services.

Take the phone numbers and addresses of hospitals or emergency rooms, go to thrift shops and learn to shop intelligently and carefully for good bargains in nice looking and well-fitting clothing, take note of mental health clinics, volunteer opportunities and employment help for those with disabilities.

Investigate subsidized public transit tickets or monthly passes. Sheltered workshops, Goodwill Industries or similar institutions frequently offer training and/or employment for people with disabilities. Take advantage of subsidized housing, free library cards if available where you can rent books, magazines, CDs and DVDs, or spend a pleasant afternoon reading in their Reading Rooms. Get help from volunteer organizations or charities with budgeting and menus if necessary.

Churches sometimes offer courses by volunteers where you can prepare a number of meals under supervision in their kitchens and take the meals home at a nominal cost. Religious institutions such as the Salvation Army are comforting to attend and a good resource for those who are looking for spirituality and friendship.

There's a section in the next chapter of this book to jot down resources available in your own community or country. You may think of many more not mentioned here. This chapter is meant only to offer suggestions and to get you thinking how you may live an optimal life at nominal cost.

Caregiving/Self Care Checklist

1. EMERGENCY NUMBERS

_____

_____

_____

2. MEDICAL HISTORY LOG

_____

_____

_____

3. MEDICATIONS LOG

_____

_____

_____

4. IMPORTANT DOCUMENTS

_____

_____

_____

5. IMPORTANT PHONE NUMBERS AND ADDRESSES

_____

_____

_____

6. CARE FACILITIES IF NECESSARY

_____

_____

7. DOCTORS' NAMES AND NUMBERS (SEE EMERGENCY NUMBERS ABOVE)

_____

_____

_____

8. NEXT OF KIN

_____

_____

_____

9. FINANCIAL EXPENSES LOG
Rent/mortgage monthly

_____

_____

Utilities (list)

_____

_____

Groceries monthly

_____

_____

Medical

_____

_____

Credit cards

_____

_____

Debts

_____

_____

Other bills

_____

_____

Entertainment

_____

Other (list)

10. ANY SPECIAL INSTRUCTIONS, RESOURCES OR NOTES

Afterword

Thank you, gentle reader, for accompanying us on this journey. If you're one who is like us, please take our hand and together we'll hike up that great mountain called Life.

If you're a physician or a therapist, a family member or a friend, we hope your understanding is illuminated a little more by taking this path with us through these pages.

In the words of Charles Dickens, God bless us, one and all. May you find joy, peace and friendship to guide you throughout this new adventure: approaching the subconscious and conquering it.

About The Authors

We are Austin Mardon, PhD, CM (Order of Canada) and Kenna Mary McKinnon, BA, both diagnosed with paranoid schizophrenia.

We have co-authored for your consideration a nonfiction book about our journey with schizophrenia, which is also well researched and suitable for therapists or family practitioners as a reference book. It includes the latest treatments and research as well as personal vignettes and suggestions which a client or caregiver will find extremely helpful. The book focuses on hope and positive outcomes.

Kenna McKinnon is a freelance writer/photographer and self-employed businesswoman who has lived successfully with schizophrenia for many years.

Kenna was born on October 23, 1944 in Toronto, Ontario and presently lives in Edmonton, Alberta. She obtained a Bachelor of Arts degree with Distinction from the University of Alberta in 1975. She has three wonderful adult children, two sons and a daughter, and three grandsons.

Although her degree is in Anthropology (with a minor in Psychology), Kenna has spent her life writing. She enjoys exploring the psychology of the human condition, especially when the accompanying human is dropped into complex and unusual circumstances.

Her Young Adult/Middle Grade SF novel, SPACEHIVE, published by *Imajin Books*, is available at Amazon in both eBook and trade paperback, and at Chapters Westside in Edmonton, Alberta.

BENJAMIN AND RUMBLECHUM is a young reader's chapter book. It was co-authored with Emma Shirley Brinson and has been accepted by *Diamond Heart Press* in California. *Benjamin and Rumblechum* will be published in April 2013.

Kenna is a member of The Writers Guild of Alberta, the Canadian Authors' Association, and Alumni Association - University of Alberta.

Kenna has been published in numerous journals in Canada and the USA including WestWord, SZ Magazine, BP Magazine, Alberta Caregiver, the Edmonton Journal, Spotlight on Recovery and many others. A complete publication list is found on her website and on her Amazon author page.

Kenna was diagnosed in 1978 with schizophrenia, is an Edmonton based freelance writer and has owned her own medical transcription business since 1999. She has a BA with Distinction from the University of Alberta (1975).

Dr. Austin Mardon, diagnosed in 1992 at the age of 30 with paranoid schizophrenia, has spoken extensively in Canada on the topic and co-authored numerous books. He received the Order of Canada in 2007 for his advocacy on behalf of those who are diagnosed with schizophrenia. He lives in Edmonton, Alberta with his wife Catherine.

Kenna McKinnon, BA

Austin Mardon, PhD, CM (Order of Canada)

References

Twitter - [@KennaMcKinnon](https://twitter.com/#!/KennaMcKinnon)

Blog – http://KennaMcKinnonAuthor.com/

Facebook - http://www.facebook.com/KennaMcKinnonAuthor

Other books by Kenna McKinnon:

- SpaceHive
- Benjamin & Rumblechum
- Den of Dark Angels
- Short Circuit and Other Geek Stories
- Discovery: A Collection of Poetry
- Bigfoot Boy: Lost on Earth
- Blood Sister

Made in the USA
Middletown, DE
25 April 2023

29442707R00086